Peace In My Mind

Also by Kelly R. Jackson

Temporarily Disconnected
A perspective on the decline of Black relationships and
families

and

Scenes From The Blue Book:
Poetry, Reflection and the Spoken Mind

Peace In My Mind

The journey to find ourselves while embracing who we are

by

Kelly R. Jackson

iUniverse, Inc.
New York   Bloomington

Peace In My Mind
The journey to find ourselves while embracing who we are

iUniverse books may be ordered through booksellers or by contacting:

iUniverse
1663 Liberty Drive
Bloomington, IN 47403
www.iuniverse.com
1-800-Authors (1-800-288-4677)

ISBN: 978-1-4401-3426-5 (pbk)
ISBN: 978-1-4401-3427-2 (ebk)

Printed in the United States of America
iUniverse rev. date: 3/31/09

Table Of Contents

Foreword

The title of this book, Peace In My Mind, reaches out to all people. In our own way, we all seek peace within ourselves. As you read this book, you will see the many ways people seek that "elusive" peace. Many turn to drugs, multiple relationships (at the same time), and sexual promiscuity. We look for outside sources to provide us with peace in our own minds.

In this author's first book, *Temporarily Disconnected*, he stated many reasons why we are disconnected from family, friends, co-workers, associates and, most of all, God. This peace discussed in this book comes when we: (1) Know God, (2) Know to whom we belong, and (3) Know who we are.

As you read Chapters 4-6 (please don't skip ahead), you will begin to see some of the ways to begin your journey towards peace. There are many barriers that can keep us from the peace in our own minds that God intended us to have with ourselves and others. But there is still hope.

"For He (God) is our peace, who hath made us one, and hath broken down the middle wall of partition between us"
- Ephesians 2:14

So there is no longer a need for us to be disconnected because God has broken down the walls. So as you read *Peace In My Mind*, enjoy it, learn from it and take an inventory of yourself.

Real peace begins within and shows on the outside. If you are looking for perfect peace, it can only be found through God.

> *"Thou will keep him in perfect peace, whose mind is stayed on thee (God); because he trusteth in thee"* – Isaiah 26:3

May God grant you peace in your mind as you read this book.

Annie Jackson-Loritts

Acknowledgments

There are so many people that I can acknowledge as I submit to you my third book. To those that have supported all of my work so far, I deeply appreciate it and I thank you from the bottom of my heart. All of the words of encouragement, the emails and the support of the website is what keeps me going and keeps me believing that I'm on the right path and doing the right thing.

To my dear mother. My rock, my heart, my soul and truly my best girl. What would I ever do without you in my corner? You are everything to me. It is an honor being your son and even more of an honor that you see even a little bit of yourself in me. I carry your teachings with me everywhere I go. You will always be in my heart and I thank you for making my dream come true by contributing the Foreword to this project. I just wanted the world to get a glimpse of the woman that I can never stop talking about. You've made me so proud. I love you mom.

To all of the members of the Flowers/Jones/McFolley family that showed me so much love and support at the family reunion, I thank you. The love that I felt that day can never be measured. I'm so proud to be a descendent of this great family and I will always do my best to represent the family name with dignity and honor. Thank you again.

To Ms. Kishau, thank you, thank you, thank you. You are the definition of friendship. From listening to whatever ideas may be rolling around in my head to dealing with my stubbornness. I know it's not always easy on KJ Street, but you just keep on driving. Thanks for making me believe that I can conquer the world, even when I don't feel like it and I'd rather just conquer my futon and the remote control. Thanks for reminding me that people are listening, even when I feel like I'm just talking out loud and no one's really paying attention. Thanks for listening, even though I ramble on sometimes to the point where you don't know what the heck I'm talking about anymore. And most of all, thank you for feeding me! You are appreciated Kish Kish.

Kelly

Introduction

Have you ever looked at yourself in the mirror and saw more than what appeared to be there? Have you ever looked into that same mirror and saw less than what should be there? Have you ever looked at that reflection and saw two sides of yourself? Some of you said yes to those questions, and some of you said no. Whether you said yes or no, there are probably two sides that exist inside of you. One may be good, and one may be bad. One may be a dark side, and one may be a lighter side. One may be your day personality, and one may be your night time personality. Lastly, one may be your earthly self, and one may be your spiritual self.

In this book, I would like to share with you some of the things that I saw when I looked into my mirror. When I finally decided to try my hand at being an author, I wasn't quite sure how any of it would turn out. I knew I had a few thoughts that I wanted to share with the world, but I wasn't sure if I would be able to concentrate on any one thing long enough to complete a book. Some of those books out there are pretty thick and I didn't know if I was ready to be a part of that world. However, after making the big leap, I couldn't be happier with my decision.

This is my third book and I feel that I've come a long way since my first book, *Temporarily Disconnected*. That book was like my open letter to the black community. My second book was the book my mother always wanted me to do, a poetry book called *Scenes From The Blue Book: Poetry, Reflection and the Spoken Mind*. In both books, I revealed some very personal things about myself to the world. But what makes this book so different is the way that it's written. One could say that the first half was written by my "earthly self", and the second half was written by my "spiritual self" (these two "people" are explained in more detail in Chapter 2). As I've already stated, I feel that all of us are operating under at least two different personalities. *Peace In My Mind* attempts to address my personalities to some degree. If *Temporarily Disconnected* was my open letter to the black community, then in some ways, *Peace In My Mind* is my open letter to myself.

When I first started writing *Peace In My Mind*, it was supposed to be something on the lighter side. In fact, there was even a different working title. *Temporarily Disconnected* was so serious in its subject matter that I wanted to give people a glimpse into a different side of me. I wanted to showcase more of my personality. Not only am I of the belief that there truly are two sides to all of us, I think that some of us, myself included, are working on more than that. I also wanted people to know that though situations may seem dire for us sometimes, it's still okay to laugh every now and then.

But as I was writing one book, I prepared myself to work on another book at the same time. During that time, I noticed that while one of the books did tend to be on the lighter side and showcase more of my sense of humor, there were still other things of a serious nature on my mind. They were things that very well could've been in the first book, but rather than write a 20 chapter book, I held some things back. But those things that I held back still needed to be said. Not sure how I would handle this situation, I received some advice from an unlikely source.

Upon learning that her uncle had written his first book, my niece Olivia asked a simple question. Well, she asked two. The first thing she asked was when she could she have some money. However, her second question was the more important and most likely to be answered question. She asked me was I going to do a series of books. A series. I hadn't thought of that. At that point, as far as I knew, I was only doing *Temporarily Disconnected* and the poetry book. But from the mouth of one special child, I came to realize that I'll be an author from now on.

Still, when I started writing some of the more serious chapters, I was writing them with the mindset that they would be in a different book. Maybe the second book in that "series". But as I found myself writing what I felt were two books at one time, I began to feel that all of these chapters may belong together. It's a strange mix of comedy, seriousness, reflection and emotion. It may or may not be confusing to the reader, but it's actually an accurate description of my personality, which mirrors my collection of music, my most prized possession this side of my son. You really never know what you're gonna get from me. In fact, I'm not even sure when I wake up in the mornings.

In creating what eventually became *Peace In My Mind*, I came to understand that there is no separating all of those different sides of me, so there probably shouldn't be any separating of the two sides of this book. Sure, there is a lighter side to me, but there's also a serious side to me. Over the last few years, I have made an attempt to do away with some of the old and unproductive ways that I have. There have been tragedies, such as Hurricane Katrina, that have reminded me and others of how fragile life can be. As a result, I've tried even harder than usual to become a better and more spiritual human being. As you will see in this book, I'm not all the way there yet and I have no illusions that I am. As much as I may have wanted to separate these two sides of one coin, they probably belong together. I wrote a poem called "Gemini" for my last book that reflected the fact that I recognize these two entities. For those that didn't get my poetry book, shame on you. But I've included the poem in this book anyway.

What I also figured out was that if I really wanted to give the reader a better idea of what I see when I look in my mirror, I needed to show them all of me. Granted, this book isn't all about me, as I still attempt to hold that mirror up to all people. There are still things in our dating world that need correction, our friendship world, our personal world and our spiritual world. The reason I chose the title *Peace In My Mind* is because those two sides of us do tend to be at war sometimes. Although we will sometimes acknowledge that some of our ways need to be done away with, we should also acknowledge that some of them need to be embraced because they may never go away. To use myself as an example, there's the side of me that's a typical male. There's the side of me that hasn't settled down yet and, just like some of my friends and family, I've wondered why. There's the side of me that is forced into the dating world because I'm not married, and thus, I have to deal with dating world crap.

On the other hand, there's the spiritual side of me. That's the side that I, and those of you reading this, most need to adhere to, but we're not always doing that. That's the side of me that people don't know about unless they spend a lot of time with me. I'm not sure that's right, but it is what it is. Some of it can be blamed on my past and some of it can be blamed on the fact that no matter what people think of me, most times, I'm willing to remain silent and let them think whatever they want to think. I never have and never will be caught up in another's perception of me. If they choose to judge from a distance rather than getting to know me, then I'll let them.

My spiritual side is also the side of me that questions the absence of Jesus in our everyday lives and in our Sunday morning messages. That's the side of me that's always looking to improve on Kelly and make him a better father, a better son, a better brother, a better uncle, a better friend and someday, a good husband. I am on the road to being a better person each day. That mountain exits for all of us and from my perspective, if we ever reach the top, then we shall see Heaven. But no matter what, all sides of me need to work in concert to create a better me.

The first half of this book covers some things that I've discussed on certain levels with members of the opposite sex for years. I've been questioned for years about why I haven't gotten married. I don't mind people asking me questions, but they always ask me as if I haven't tried to find a wife. I feel that anyone that thinks that I don't have a desire to get married doesn't know me at all. To take that a step further, they have no idea about the dating scene either. It's a hard knock life for women *and* men these days. I could marry tomorrow, but all that would result in are more questions like, "Why in the hell did he marry *her*?" Hopefully, I've provided some insight in this book if you didn't get any from the first one.

The first half also covers the side of me that likes to be a regular guy. I respect and understand the ladies a lot more than most men I know, but I still love sports and movie violence, too. I have a deep love for my television and I'm constantly under the impression that my space in being threatened. I'm living proof that one can write and express his feelings and still be a "real man" that likes real things. Even though some of us need to change some of our ways and work on being better people, there's still some things about us that are just who we are. Some of those things can be funny sometimes, some of those things need to be done away with and some of those things just need to be embraced because, as I said, they may never change.

The second half of this book takes you in a different direction. While the secular side of me is acknowledged, the spiritual side of me needs to take the lead for good. As I stated in the last paragraph, there are things about me that may never change, but there are also things about me that *need* to change. There are things about all of us that need to change. Though we exist in the flesh, we need to be mindful of the fact that succumbing to the flesh too often and in the wrong instances can place our souls in jeopardy. I know that I haven't been an awful person. In fact, my mom tells me often that I'm a good son. But no matter how you've been living, there's always room for improvement. We must remain humble.

For some of you reading this book, you may prefer one half to the other, and that's okay. For example, if you're still single, then the first half of this book may be something that you can relate to. However, if you're one that's on a quest for more spiritual growth, maybe reading about my current journey may be something that you can relate to. If not or if you're one of my older readers, the second half of this book may be something that you can relate to. I encourage you to read the chapter titles and decide where you want to go first. Not that I can do anything about it, but you're more than welcome to read the book in reverse order, second half first, and the first half second.

Ultimately, I hope that you enjoy the book in its entirety. I feel that there's something here for everyone and as usual, it's my hope that you may see yourself in my work. It's always my hope that people may be inspired to change through reading about my quest for the very same thing. It is a strange ride, but my life has been somewhat of a strange ride and this was just one way of me sharing it with you. Sometimes I may talk in third person, but don't be alarmed. Maybe "Gemini" will explain some of that. I just do it to make you laugh. But more than anything, I want you all to see the growth in me. Enjoy

KJ

Gemini

I've been trying to get in touch with my inner Gemini

'Cause I see the similarities between him and I

Special baby boy 'cause his mama said so

Put the pen to the paper, now I'm ready to blow

And we'll keep this thing movin' 'til the world sings my song

And 'cause duality exists, we don't always get along

My conflicts are real, I'm tryin' to right my wrongs

So we write in third person when we can't get along

Arrogance is fleeting, but when put to the test

He won't hesitate to tell you that he's one of the best

Too brash or too confident, it's all the same

But at the end of the day, his humility reigns

Recognition of the gifts that God has bestowed

Is the only way the gifts can continue to flow

I pray to God every night that he lights our way

'Cause my dark side twin will try to lead me astray

When I drive the Big Dog he makes me drive too fast

He makes me lust for a girl that's much too fast

When I should be home, he keeps me out half the night

He uses four-letter words when we ain't been treated right

But when my dark side threatens to claim my soul

It's the strength of my character that takes control

We're tryin' to make it right before we get too old

We're tryin' our best to find the right body to hold

Embracing spirituality is what we must learn

As the dark side will lead to a permanent burn

Though our dark side tends to be a lot of fun

What you lose is most times worth more that what you've won

In the face of all that's wrong, we must take a stand

And build the foundation of a better man

Though duality exists, we must take control

While accepting that the two halves make us whole

Come to terms with who you are 'cause it's what you must do

And embrace the Gemini that exists in you

KJ

Chapter 1

"Kelly, why aren't you married?"

Well, we may as well just get right to it, huh? This question has followed me since, well, it seems like forever. It seems to me that as soon as we're able to leave home and be on our own, someone's trying to rush us off into marriage. This probably doesn't happen as much with women as it does with men because women are usually the ones applying that pressure. Whether it's your mom, your sister, your aunt or your girlfriend, there's usually some woman, somewhere pressuring some poor young man into marriage. And women don't discriminate with that pressure. They actually pressure themselves, and even one another. To use that off-color comment that former sports analyst and current moron Jimmy "The Greek" Snyder used when describing why he thought blacks were superior to whites in some sports, women are "just bred that way".

From the time that they're little girls, they're told that they have to grow up, get married and have a family. It's passed on to them as some sort of rite of passage or career goal. There's some good and some bad in women being taught that from the age of five, and we'll get to that in a moment. But men are wired completely different. Yes, some of us are looking for the right woman, and that takes a little longer than it used to. For all of the women out there that don't buy that, then you're just not paying as much attention to your "colleagues "as you should. However, some of us evade marriage like a deadbeat dad evades the Friend of the Court. You'll have to arrest us to get what you want out of us. But no matter which side of that fence that a man is on, the question will always be there, even if he's explained himself over and over again: Why aren't you married?

Now, I hate to disappoint some of the readers that know me personally, but the title of this chapter is a bit misleading. This *whole* chapter won't be about why my tuxes have all been for proms, military balls and groomsman duty thus far. The reasons that I'm minus Mrs. Jackson these days will be spelled out to *some* degree at the end of this chapter. What I'd like to share with you in the beginning of this chapter is why I feel that most men and women have trouble jumping the broom these days.

There are many different perspectives that a man has when it comes to marriage. I know, I know, a lot of you thought that we only had one: A man lives a few years as a bachelor and then he gets married or he dies, and the feeling is pretty much the same no matter which one he chooses. A lot of us do think that way, but not all of us. Some of us view marriage as a beautiful thing. Some of us view marriage as a sacred thing. Some of us actually do look forward to getting married, having a few babies and living happily ever after. And then, there are those of us who think it's a curse. Depending on who you're involved with throughout your life and how you were raised, all of these perspectives could probably be justified in one way or another.

I believe how one views marriage, whether male or female, depends on the type of individuals they've come in contact with throughout their lives. For example, if you came from a broken home, you may be down on marriage. At the same time, a broken home could make one more determined to make a marriage work. If you've dealt with a lot of cheating in relationships, that could make you leery about making the big leap. If every man you've ever dealt with was abusive, how could you really be expected to look forward to spending the rest of your life with one? If every woman that you've ever dealt with was nothing but a gold digger that never appreciated you beyond the money that you made, how could you be looking forward to a lifetime working in the salt mines just to make her comfortable?

For men, the commitment thing always has been, and to some degree, always will be an issue. Even if you're dealing with a man that's looking forward to getting married, he still understands that, on some level, he's giving up something. It may be his perceived freedom (we sometimes don't realize that if you're in *any* kind of relationship with a woman, whether real or imagined, you're never really free), his friends, his space, his dog, his season tickets if she's not a sports fan, his sense of well-being, or his right to eat whatever he wants in bed, no matter what time of day or night, and watch endless amounts of sports and/ or nude or semi-nude women parade across the television screen in a seemingly endless loop, while never once compromising his position as lord and ruler of the remote control. Not that I have any experience with any of this, but I'm just sayin'.

On the other hand, things are different between men and women these days. The reasons that I mentioned above used to be the only reasons that a man was afraid to commit to a woman. These days, women are just as promiscuous as men are usually thought to be, so it would be wise for a man to slow down and take his time. I guess what I'm saying to the ladies is, it's bad enough that we were already manufacturing reasons not to be at the church on time, then you guys had to go and legitimized our bridal boycott by picking up some of our bad habits.

"You tryin' to set me up..."

Back in the day, when a woman wanted a man to marry her, unless she was straight out of *Thin Line Between Love and Hate* or *Fatal Attraction*, she was usually trying to do a good thing in a man's life. Most men don't really get this, but if a good woman wants to marry you, she's not just trying to "tie you down", she's trying to save your life. When we're off and running far and fast through the jungle (the streets, night clubs, some other woman's house) before the jungle hunter that *is* your woman hunts you down, she's not really trying to kill you. She's almost like Greenpeace or something. Yeah, she wants to capture you, but only to take you to a safer place. She realizes that all of that running around without any protection or structure will soon lead to our demise somehow. A good woman realizes that there's a difference between living and surviving. Left all alone for all of their days, most men will survive. But when you have a good woman in your life, you're alive. You do more than survive.

If we could just learn once again to look past our fears, we as men could once again learn to see the merits of marriage. We could once again learn to see the benefits of it. It's not solely about having someone in the home to take the place of our mothers and pick up after us. It's not solely about having someone fulfill our dreams of having a son to play catch with or a daughter to agonize over. It's about finding that special someone to build a life with. Note: I did not say someone to live with, I said someone to <u>build a life</u> with.

Now, I'm not going to rehash my first book by going over all of the dating do's and don'ts that can lead one to the wrong partner. But in my opinion, a lot of the fear that we as men have stems from the wrong choices that we make in the dating game. We're okay as long as we're only dating these women that we're not compatible with, and we're willing to ignore all of that incompatibility. But as soon as someone mentions a jeweler, we wanna point out all of the differences we have with this evil and suspect woman. All of a sudden, she's a gold digger. All of a sudden, she's not a good cook. All of a sudden, you don't know if she was raised with the same values that you were raised with. All of a sudden, all of her male friends *are* a problem. All things that were always true, but you were willing to ignore them because you guys were only dating, she was fine and looked good on your arm, and she was good in bed. All of the pitfalls of the shallow mind.

As it always is with everything in KJWorld, I'm not just pointing fingers. I'm living this dream (or rather, nightmare) right along with my brothas. I've lived some of this same nonsense that I'm pointing out now. How else do you figure that I'd be an authority on it? It's so easy to fall into a rut in many phases of our lives, and this seems to be one of the most common. You date and you date and you date, but as soon as someone looks up and recognizes that, after 12 years, we're no longer just "feeling each other out", we're wasting each other's lives, we wanna put the brakes on. It really is as simple as not buying the cow when you can get the milk for free.

Men will only make life changing moves when inspired to or when forced to. 90% is force. We have a boardroom mentality. If you're trying to convince your boss that your project or idea will save the company, he'll carve out part of his day, and you'll have a certain amount of time to "wow" that man. If you don't get it done in that allotted amount of time, then all is lost. You may never get a chance again. However, if you were to buy up all of the company's stock in a hostile takeover and implement your plan, your boss would be forced to comply or he'd have to look for employment elsewhere. So, it should be upon all women to have a game plan.

Now, understand what I'm saying ladies. Don't have a plan for his money. Don't look for ways to "trap" him. Don't have a "scheme". To be blunt, when I say have a game plan, I mean have yo' (fill in the blank) together. If you're a real woman and you want a real man in your life, you don't have to trick, scheme or sucker him into wanting you. Just by being yourself, you can show him what he could have in his life for many days to come if he simply had *his* (fill in the blank) together. A real woman doesn't need all of those games to get someone to the altar. A real woman is so appealing to *all* men that they either want to do better so that they can have her hand in marriage, or they're so afraid of the challenge, they won't bother wasting too much of her time if they can't cut it. Just by being in her presence, a real woman can make you wanna live a better life. That's the inspiration end of the deal. If you're an extraordinary woman and that part of you is on display for all to see, any man, real or otherwise, will take notice. By doing that, a woman goes from having to put up with any ol' knucklehead to having her choice. From there, if a man happens to be said knucklehead, he's knows that if he is to have you, then a change is in order.

Now, as I said, that's the inspiration end of the deal. Remember, 90% is force. Again, I'm not talking about those ways that women have "forced" men into marriage before. False pregnancies aside, if you have to force a man to be with you, then maybe you should consider someone else. But when I say that some men have to be forced into change, I mean that there are many instances when a man can clearly see that a particular move is what's in his best interest, and he still won't make it. Either because he's too lazy, too scared or it's really bothering him that it wasn't his idea.

Some of that stubbornness that we have as little boys when we refuse to take naps or baths will carry over into adulthood, and for some of my brethren, the baths are still a point of concern. How you expect any woman to marry you under those circumstances, I'll never know. But, I digress. As I said before, we're like animals in the jungle. We don't think in terms of quality of life as far as marriage is concern, we think in terms of survival. It's sad, but true. We don't always look to extract happiness from a marriage. We just hope to live through it in the same way we did The Bush Administration. If a woman paints us into a corner and shows us why we can't survive without them, we will respond in the name of survival.

You have to make it make sense to a man. This is difficult, as talking to a man really can be like talking to a brick wall. We can understand things as complex as football, the Three Stooges, the flux capacitor and how it allowed Marty McFly to travel back in time in *Back To The Future*, or why we believe that any one of those *Terminator* movies could've really happened, but you'd have to beat us down to make us understand how the right woman can bring us the kind of happiness that can only be rivaled by the birth of your children. Women have tricked themselves into believing that all they have to do is make him fall in love, and the hard part is over. Believe it or not, ladies, that's the easy part. Sure, it may take him 4 or 5 months to *say* "I love you", but it's been there. You guys are always the last to know. Even the so-called hard man is willing to love a woman. But getting us to drink the Jim Jones kool-aid that is marriage? A whole different ballgame.

A woman has to take the time to figure out what a man really needs. And they can't fall into the trap of thinking that we're all the same and there's some cookie-cutter pattern that they can all follow to have any man. True, there are some very basic similarities that all men have, like the love of cooked food. But that, along with some other basics, are things that will make a man content, and sometimes satisfied. But the key to longevity is true happiness. People who are content or just satisfied in relationships will eventually drift apart, and sometimes, drift to other people.

When people come undone, it's usually because one or both are no longer happy in their current situation. From those basic similarities that men do have, a woman must find out what really makes her man happy. She must find out what he values most if she wants to reach him. But more importantly, when she finds that out, she must look within herself and be <u>completely</u> honest. She has to ask her self some critical questions: Do I have what he needs to really make him happy? And if the answer is no, she must ask herself, am I willing and capable of giving that man what he needs?

Again, I don't wanna go back to the first book too much, but so many times people want to rush men off into marriage when they just aren't ready. This is never good. I'm not in any way suggesting that women wait around forever for a man to get ready. I'm not in any way suggesting that women not ask questions and try to gain some sort of perspective on when things will move forward or whether or not they will at all. I'm not in any way suggesting that a woman shouldn't do certain things to help move the process along a little bit. I'm just saying that men don't respond well to relationship pressure, and making him commit sooner than he wants to can backfire. Sometimes, you have to let things take their natural course. Don't play yourself out and waste years of your life waiting around for some man to decide whether or not he wants to be with you, but don't lean on him so hard that you force him to walk away because you won't give him time or space. Marriage is supposed to be a lifetime commitment, and something that takes up the rest of your life shouldn't be rushed into.

30 going on 90

Speaking of rushing, what is the real reason that we feel that we should be married by a certain age? Again, this isn't as much a man problem as it is a woman's, but it's an issue nonetheless. I've noticed that if a woman isn't married with 2.5 kids by the age of 30, she immediately goes running for the panic button. I've always recognized 30 as a turning point in one's life, but we as a society have turned 30 into some sort of death march. I've noticed that if a woman reaches 30 and she's not married, her next thought is to drive to a bridge or the closest gun shop and end it all. This has always struck me as absurd, but yet it continues to be an issue. The only question I have is, why? Why has this become the most important thing a woman feels she must accomplish by the age of 30?

I was once told by an ex-girlfriend that if she turned 30 and I hadn't proposed, we would've been through. Luckily for her, by the time she was 30, she was already done with me and my unbending knee. It would've been a shame to have to end it all on her 30th. I could see her birthday party now. Everyone giving her gifts while she waits for my proposal. Meanwhile, I'd be standing there with a "You're not the boss of me!" t-shirt on. It always struck me as odd that she was more concerned about me proposing by a certain point in her life than she was about me being the right man for the job. In my opinion, had we made it to her 30th birthday, it would've made more sense for her to look at us and decide if it were worth it to go forward, as opposed to demanding some sort of further commitment.

As I said, 30 is a time for reflection. It's one of those points in one's life when you take a look around and take stock of your life. During that period, if you aren't married, you might ask yourself why. And the reality is you may come up with a number of reasons why you aren't. Some of them may be your fault, and a lot of them may not be. But whatever the case may be, and this is especially true with women, you have to be willing to accept the fact that, in this climate, you may not be married by the age of 30. And, whether women like it or not or understand it or not, it's okay.

A lot of this goes back to how we define our lives. So many of us define our lives by our accomplishments. Now, it depends on the individual as to what you may call an accomplishment.

For some of us, it's success on the job. For some of us, it's having a big house and expensive cars. For some of us, it's helping out our fellow man in the community. For some men, it's not about having the *right* woman on their arm, but rather the prettiest or the hottest or the most Coke bottle-esque woman on their arm. For some women, it's not about having the *right* man on their arm, but rather the richest or the flyest or the most handsome or the most well endowed man on their arm. However, for some of us, it's about being married and having just about any particular individual on our arm.

When planning out your life, there's nothing wrong with placing expectations upon yourself. There's nothing wrong with wanting to have this kind of life, with that kind of job, with this kind of house, living in that kind of neighborhood. But one shouldn't view getting married as an accomplishment. One can view *having* a successful marriage as an accomplishment, but not the act of simply getting married. In fact, I'm not sure it should even be a goal as much as it should be something that one has a desire for. Working toward marriage with an individual is one thing, but working toward marriage with whomever by a certain number, come hell or Hurricane Katrina, is a whole different matter altogether.

It seems to me that, at some point in a woman's life, certain individual accomplishments begin to take a back seat to marriage. Now, that's not all wrong in its proper context. For example, if a woman decides to marry and have children and she chooses to put her career on hold to take care of her family, then that's fine, as long as it's her choice. But when a woman begins to lump her *desire* to be married in with her career goals in life and begins to treat them as if they're one in the same, then I think there's a problem.

Know that when I'm saying these things, I'm not trying to downplay the importance of wanting to be married and having a family. Know that I'm not saying that all a person should be about is money and career. If you've ever read anything that I've written, you know that's far from any belief that I have. I've just always had a hard time understanding why the only thing it seems that some of these women feel that they *must* do by the age of 30 is get married.

Women have to move beyond the idea that there's a "stigma" attached to being single after the age of 30. The only time that there's a stigma is when we place it there. If we as men and women could simply stop trying to live up to everyone else's expectations and set standards and rules for our own lives, we'd all be a lot better off. In fact, if we had a melding of the male and female ideals on this, we'd probably all be a lot better off.

Most single men could care less when someone tells us how we *should* be married by now. Even when we're 45, still in the club wearing Brut by Faberge and this is literally sound advice, we still move to the beat of our own drum. We could lose a fiancé and simply treat it like a lost sense of pride and self esteem. It'll be a few months before we really noticed that they're gone, and another two before we realize how much we need them. Although this form of emotional blindness is most times to our detriment, women could benefit from this ability to tune a deaf ear to those who dare to tell you where you should or shouldn't be in your personal life. No matter what some may think, there is no *perfect* time to get married, only a *right* time. And it's up to each individual to determine what that time is in their lives.

While we as men need to stop running so fast to get away from the long arm of the law, women need to slow down and take their time. This isn't the days of old when those expectations made some sort of sense. There's a lot more that women can accomplish these days as individuals before even thinking about getting married and having kids. Men have always thought this way. I don't understand why women won't follow. Unless the dude is sorry, men have always wanted to have a few things in place before they proposed. It just makes sense.

In days past, women counted on men to be the bread winners while they stayed at home and raised the kids. In that world, it made sense for a woman to get married early on. If she wasn't going to work and she wasn't going to school, why not get hitched and make some babies? But Fred and Wilma Flintstone have long since moved off the scene (i.e., this isn't the Stone Ages, for all of you that didn't get that). This is a new day. Women have to stop attaching their successes or failures in life to whether or not they have a man. Have that life, have that career, and when the time is right, have that husband and have that family. Some things in life you can force and get away with it. If you force yourself into marriage, more times than not, you'll have problems. Men understand this, but maybe a little too well sometimes. We should only marry because it's the right time and the right person, not because we're "old" and it's expected.

Now, the flip side to this is the biological clock of women. The general thought is that they want to get married when they're young enough to have babies. That's a very valid point. If you want to have a couple of babies, it'd probably be wise to close the deal before your 45th birthday. Having said that, women are having babies a lot later in life these days. Science has moved along quite nicely in the last, oh, 100 years. The old thinking that a woman having babies after 30 is sure to die some horrible death is long gone. It's not only safer than it used to be, it's a lot more common. Does that mean that every woman should wait until she's in her mid to late 30's to have a baby? No, not if you don't have to.

What it does mean is that if you're 30 and you're not married and you haven't had your 2.5, it's not only okay, it ain't over yet. You still have an opportunity to live out that dream. When I mentioned this to a friend of mine once, she said to me that her only concern was the age and generation gap that she'd experience with her child. Again, a valid concern. However, my mom had me when she was 32 and she's been my best friend for most of my life. To me, that comes down to parenting and how involved you wanna be in your child's life. The gap between parent and child isn't always generational. It's usually just a lack of involvement. The more involved you are, the shorter the bridge between you and your child. When we fall in love and there's an age gap, we're quick to say that "age ain't nothin' but a number". Why not apply that same thinking to your child?

"Know your role, and shut your mouth…"

Before I end this chapter, a quick aside. When we do finally come to an agreement to move from man and woman to husband and wife, why is there ever any confusion about how the wedding should go? Now granted, I've had a lot of pages of opinions here for someone who's never even been engaged, let alone married, but this one I really feel strongly about. Men have no place in wedding preparation. And that's the way it's supposed to be. Now, even though I haven't been married, I've been in a couple of weddings. The most involved I've ever been was in my friend's wedding. Having been in on the ground floor of one of these things, I've wondered why any man would ever want to be involved any more than he had to. Other than being control freaks, I can't think of any other reasons. Having watched firsthand all of the things that go into it, I cringed at the thought of the day that I finally will say "I do". I mean, picking out china patterns? My goodness. Just the thought almost makes me too sleepy to finish this chapter.

A lot of men think that because, in most cases, some of their money is involved, they should be involved and have something to say. First of all, let me tell you that there are going to be a lot of things concerning that woman that will involve your money that you'll have little to no control over. I'll quote Will Ferrell from the movie *Anchorman: The Legend Of Ron Burgundy*. When telling Christina Applegate's character why he thought men were smarter than women, he simply said, "It's science". If you've even seen that movie, then you know that Will said it in a tone and with a look on his face that suggested that because "it's science", there absolutely nothing that you can do about it. The fact that you're footing part of the bill and you're one half of the guests of honor means nothing. This is just one of those things that men should just leave to the "professionals".

KJ has one very simple philosophy on why men should just make sure they're on time, and make sure that they're standing wherever they're told to stand. My thought is that most women have been planning their weddings from the time they were teenagers. Colors and all. Because of that fact, the magnitude of the event, and the impact that it will have on their lives, they will remember just about every detail of it for the rest of their lives.

They won't remember that you told them two weeks ago that you had to work late on the 3rd and that you won't be able to make dinner at the in-laws, but they'll remember that wedding day in great detail for the rest of their lives. IN GREAT DETAIL, FELLAS! For the most part, all we'll remember is that we were there. The rest will pretty much be a blur. Family, friends, a minister, a flower girl, drunken relatives at the reception and slightly above average food, all mixed together so well, that it all seems like that dream sequence on *Dallas* when Bobby Ewing was dead for a year, and it turned out that it was all a Victoria Principal dream (that was just a ridiculous day in television history).

Because this day is so important to women, we should allow them to have what they want, the way they want. Too often, men get involved and completely screw up the dream for many a bride out there. All because we feel that our opinion should be heard. But, we must remember what I said. In great detail, these brides will remember this day. Whether good or bad, fellas. That's why we have to stay out of it.

Sure, women are partly responsible for us putting our grimy hands all over the sanctity of this most glorious day by asking that oh so pointless question: "Well, what do you think, honey?" A little advice ladies: Who cares what he thinks? He doesn't even care. He only answered because you asked. You think it really matters to him what patterns are on that plate? Try setting it down in front of him two weeks after you're married and you'll see how much he cares. If the plate doesn't have any food on it, then it's a waste of his time. You ask what he thinks, and he's probably forgotten what he told you right after he said it.

Now, don't get me wrong, fellas. They pretend to want us involved. You have to meet with people and go places and look at things that have something to do with the big day, and they've got you doing all of these things like it really matters what you feel.

But when she's asking you what you think about any particular thing, what she's really saying is, "Say yes to what I say yes to". Gentlemen, you must comply.

I know what you're thinking, "But KJ, I'm not a mind reader". I'm not asking you to be. However, if you plan to marry this woman, you should have a decent idea about what she will and won't go for. You should be able to fake your way through all things unpleasant by now. But if you're one of those brothas that's a little thick in the head and you don't catch on too fast, if you screw up and say the wrong thing, you can always get back by saying these words: "You know what honey, you were right, and I was wrong. Let's go with your suggestion".

Now, remember guys, you don't wanna wear that one out. There will be days when being that agreeable will not only backfire on you, it'll get you in trouble if she thinks you're not paying attention. However, that shouldn't be the case here. If anything, she'll appreciate the lack of resistance. Just remember guys, it's her day. Don't ruin it with your desire to be heard. Just sit back, and let it happen to you. You'll be glad you did when she can look back on her wedding and all of the things that went wrong (because something inevitably always goes wrong) had little or nothing to do with you.

I asked you a question…

Now, with all of that said, I've decided to answer the question that this chapter asks. Kelly, why aren't you married? Well, the short answer is it's just not as simple as it used to be to find good women (sorry ladies). A lot of the answers actually do exist in some of the lines I've already written here. Whether those that wish I were married by now are willing to admit it or not, it's just harder than it used to be. It's not harder for those that are willing to settle or compromise to their detriment, but for people that want to hold on to what's important to them, it is a challenge. Marriage shouldn't be taken lightly and I do want my mother to see her baby boy get married. But I wanna do my best to make sure that she only has to see it once because I found the right woman. Not one that's perfect, but one that's perfect for me.

That in itself is quite the challenge. This is the first chapter in a two-sided book that, for all intents and purposes, has been written by two different sides of my personality. Finding someone that's compatible with that ain't no easy chore. She's gonna have to let me be me, no matter which me I decide to be that day. As I said, a lot of the answers to the question of why I'm not married exist in some of the lines of this chapter and those to come. However, I thought it would be fun if I listed a few in particular for you. To take a page from one of my all-time favorites, David Letterman, I'll end this chapter not with 10, but with my Top Five Reasons That KJ's Not Married. I know, this is all so sad, but let's read along anyway.

5. Transportation/The Mall

When you get married, more times than not, there are children in your future. If there are children in your future, chances are, there may be a minivan in your future as well. Although you can get a man to drive a minivan, he doesn't ever want it to be his primary source of transportation. Yes, it is practical, but to a man, it's never cool. Now, I sold cars for three years and I'll tell you, there's probably no smoother ride than a minivan, all luxury cars aside. But as men, we will sacrifice that comfort to be cool any day of the week. My large SUV, though gas guzzling, will more than accommodate those kids. So get back there in the third row and settle down, for God's sake!

Now, once we get in that SUV, we'll usually be off to do some shopping and it's usually at the suburbia nightmare that is the mall. If there's one thing that KJ doesn't do, it's pointless shopping. I've seen so many men being dragged from store to store in the mall by a wife all too willing to spend the next four hours trying on outfits that she doesn't plan to buy for the next month, while forcing some poor man to hold her purse while his stomach growls louder than the meanest dog you've ever seen. This is an obligation that KJ wants no part of. When I go to the mall, I go straight to what I'm looking for, buy it, get in my <u>SUV</u> and drive away. I have no desire to shop til' I drop, but most women do. The only woman that I've ever met that shares that sentiment is my mom. If I can find a woman that I can convince to *always* leave me parked in front of the TV instead of the women's section at Macy's when she feels the need to do that, then we may be on our way. Hey, I'm even willing to pay for it, as long as I'm left alone.

4. Prince/Music

Those who are well versed in KJ probably thought that this would be higher on the KJ chart. Everyone knows that I have an impressive collection of music, and none more than the offerings from a certain musician from Minneapolis. I won't get into all of the reasons I think this is the most talented individual I've ever seen. Who knows, maybe I'll write a book on that one day. But there are times when I can listen to him back to back to back, for hours and hours and hours. I've only dated two women in my lifetime that could do the same thing. Does my wife have to be able to do that? It'd be nice, but no. But what she does have to have is tolerance. Just allow me to have those moments and I promise that sooner or later, you'll come to understand why I think his music is so great. You may never be an addict like me, but you will start to get it if you don't already. I've never met a single person that didn't like at least one of his songs. Even my mom liked "Diamonds and Pearls". All I ask is a little understanding. Understand that he's one of my musical heroes. Understand that I'll zone out when listening to him. And understand that when he comes to town, I'm going. With or without you.

As far as the rest of my collection, it's very diverse. There's rock, rap, R & B, blues, jazz, gospel, reggae, oldies, you name it, and it's probably there. Except country. Just can't do it. Again, the wife doesn't have to be into all of that, but she has to have tolerance. Understand that there will be times when we'll be riding along and some sounds that may be very foreign to her may be coming out of the radio. Tolerance. And because I make it my business to be aware of music that I like *and* don't like, there will be times when we'll be riding along in her car and there will be sounds coming from her stereo that I don't quite understand. Because I respect the stereo of the driver and I demand that they do the same when riding in my truck, I won't touch the stereo. I may often be heard asking "What is this crap?", but I'll never touch your stereo. You see, I'm kind of what they call a music snob. Because my tastes are so diverse and my knowledge is extensive, nobody's music makes sense but mine. It's selfish and arrogant, true, but at least I can admit it. I've thought of going to therapy about it, but the music in the psychiatrist's office sucks.

Music is a big part of who I am. I've often said that the best gift I ever got was a radio that my cousin Sheila gave me when I was 12. It wasn't a brand new radio. It was old, the record player didn't work, and the face plate was broken so you couldn't tell what station you were listening to half the time. But it was mine. Because I was allowed to listen to what I wanted, when I wanted, I became aware of a lot of different styles of music. In a lot of ways, I feel that it helped to broaden my mind about a lot of other things in life. What my wife will have to understand is how important music has been, and still is in my life. She'll also have to understand that her music is sub-par. That's why I always drive. So that I can control the radio. All jokes aside (except about the driving, that's very true), whether I was playing it or just listening to it, music has always been significant. Again, my loves don't have to be her loves. She just needs to recognize music's place in my world. Tolerance.

3. Fear of sharing my TV/Remote

There are so many different directions I can go with this one. Now, KJ has always been sort of a TV junkie. Hell, I even worked in television for 7 years. I don't watch as many different programs as I used to, but I still watch a lot. There are a few essentials that I must have. First, there is *The Simpsons*. My love for these yellow cartoon characters is often misunderstood by most women that I've been involved with. In days past, men usually had this problem with The Three Stooges. It doesn't matter how many times I've seen these episodes of *The Simpsons*, whenever they're on, no matter what my wife wants to do, be it dinner with her folks or children's dance recitals, it's gonna wait a half hour if Bart and Homer are on the screen. The wife will have to understand.

Then, there are sports. This takes up most of my TV watching these days. During football season, I am unavailable for about 11 hours on Sundays. The only person that gets time *is* God. But after service, all bets are off, particularly during any game involving my beloved Dallas Cowboys, win, lose or draw. Imagine marrying me and finding out in the fall that the NFL *and The Simpsons* are on every Sunday. That poor woman. Throw in the fact that she'll have to sacrifice 3 hours on Saturday for Michigan football and Monday nights for whatever game is on then, and you can see what the future Mrs. Jackson is up against. I believe they call them Football Widows when the fall rolls around. If a woman doesn't have a high tolerance for all of these things, some NBA action and a lot of ESPN, I'm not sure she's the right candidate for this office.

I once had my own website and I wrote a piece called "Remote CONTROL!". It spoke about men and our relationship with the remote. You'll be able to read it in my chapter on men and all of our little quirks later in this book. Any woman that's ever dated me knows that I don't have a lot of faith in their remote handling abilities. Now, don't overreact, ladies. I'm not saying that you don't know how to push the buttons or change the channels. It's just that you guys have a propensity for stopping in all of the wrong places. Like the Lifetime Network for Women. Or the Soap Opera Network. Or any Julia Roberts movie. These things are soft and disturbing to KJ.

Sure, I've written some beautiful poetry in my day, but that's all on paper. It's not being broadcast all over the place for everyone to see. A person can read that and keep it to themselves. My wife can have the remote when I nod off, but if I wake up, its all over (and trust me, at the first sign of some teary-eyed love story or some woman scorned that seeks revenge by offing her husband on that Network for Women, I will wake up).

2. KJ's need for silence/alone time

This will probably be the toughest for any woman that I marry. I feel that I'm a pretty nice, easy going guy. However, I can be very moody. Now, when I say moody, it may not be in the way that you think. In fact, it isn't the way that a lot of people think. I'm not moody in the sense that I can be nice and then turn mean on you (although those that don't know me well, but think that they do, would disagree). I'm moody in the sense that one day I can be very talkative, and the next day I may have little or nothing to say. The complex thing for a woman to deal with in this situation is that my actual mood hasn't changed. If I'm in a good mood, you can't tell sometimes because I'm not talking.

People who go from one extreme to the other like that are sometimes thought to be in a bad mood, and most times that's not the case with me. Sometimes, I just don't feel like talking. This can be very annoying to a woman that won't stop talking to save her life. And that in turn becomes very annoying for KJ, because then I have to deal with that all too common whine "Talk to meeeeee". This also comes along with "Why don't you have anything to say to me?", and my all-time favorite, "Are you mad at me?"

Now, on the surface, these all seem like legitimate questions. But if you plan to marry a man, you should be very familiar with him and any mood swings that he may be bringing. If ever there was anything that was true of me, it's the fact that I have no problem letting anyone know when I'm angry with them.

Some would say that I'm a little too willing to let it be known for their tastes. Some would say that they would be in favor of me just internalizing sometimes like most men do, but that's what makes KJWorld so much fun. It's unlike any amusement park you've ever been to. You never know which way the rollercoaster is going. Sometimes it lulls you into a false sense of security, and then WHAM! 300 foot drop. A woman has to be willing to understand that it's gonna be quiet sometimes with me. Nobody's mad, nobody wants a divorce, nobody thinks it's time we started taking separate vacations, nobody's got a mistress and a second family hidden somewhere. I just don't have anything to say right now. Unless my team loses or Whitney and Bobby get another reality TV show. Then you won't be able to shut me up about how wrong all of that seems.

What all of this leads to is KJ's need for some alone time. This is hard to do when you're married. She wants to talk about her day and you just wanna drift away into the TV. You can see the dichotomy here. I need a woman that will understand that I need to be in another room for a while. Maybe to watch TV, maybe to think or maybe even to write another book about how she won't give me the time alone that I need. I'm willing to negotiate my coming to bed at a decent hour, although I may not be negotiating in good faith because I'm sure to break the deal. But I promise, if there's a spider to be killed or a child to be reprimanded, I'll be available. I just want the future Mrs. Jackson to be aware that there will be times when I'll walk into the house quoting Jack Nicholson as The Joker from *Batman*: "I'm gonna need a moment alone...".

1. "I'm looking for a woman like my mama"

If there was ever a reason that I've taken my time getting married, this is the one. Unless you're Eminem, most men want to marry a woman that has some of the characteristics of his mother. She doesn't have to be just like mom, but she needs to have some of those same qualities. Let's face it ladies, you don't have to have a child to end up taking care of one. Just as most women will never stop needing that father figure in their lives, most men never stop needing the nurturing that only a mother or mother figure can provide. In essence, we're both looking for the same thing. We wanna be taken care of in a manner that we've become accustomed to through the years.

Now, it should be noted that I'm talking about good parents here. If your mom wasn't the best mother in the world, it wouldn't be wise to look for a woman like that (see Eminem). Although some do wind up marrying people like their parents, even when mom and dad weren't the best (have I mentioned Eminem yet?), what I'm looking for is totally different. Considering the fact that my mom is an extraordinary woman, it would stand to reason that I may be looking for something extraordinary in my future wife.

It's been said in my family that the reason that my brothers and I haven't married is because we're trying to find a woman like my mom. My only question is, what's wrong with that? Why shouldn't we want a woman as strong, as intelligent, as multi-faceted, as spiritual, and certainly as beautiful as my mom? She's the blueprint that my brothers, my son, my nephews and certainly I should look for in a woman.

It's not just about cooking and cleaning up after us, which my mother certainly did until she taught us to do those things on our own in the name of being self sufficient. It's about the little things. Hugs when you need 'em (and mom knows when you need 'em whether you say anything or not), good sound advice (believe it or not, a man does need advice from his wife from time to time), and unconditional love and support. All the things that mom gives you. If you're thinking about the future and having any children, you want a woman that will take care of you, because if she takes care of you, she'll take care of your children.

When I look at how we were raised and all of the love that my mom gave to us, I can't help but want to marry a woman with the same make up. All of the sacrifices that she made for her children are the same sacrifices that I would like to know that my wife would make for her children. I'm not suggesting that my wife be the only one making sacrifices, I'd just like to know that I won't be the only one making sacrifices for the family. I feel that I have a lot to offer any woman that I may marry someday. Why shouldn't I be with someone that has a lot to offer me?

I'm not asking for anything that I'm not willing to give in return. If I wasn't what some woman thought I should be in order to be her husband, I wouldn't ask her to settle for less, so why should I? I have a vision of being married to a beautiful woman that I can take walks with, hold hands with and kiss on the hand affectionately as we eat lunch from the same plate in a small café somewhere. Now, if I'm willing to share food with her, you know she's special.

Sometimes, when people rush into marriage, they settle. I don't ever want that to be me. I wanna be all that my wife thought I would be, and I'm hoping that she'll be the same for me. I want it to be a union that we've both waited our entire lives for. I've dated some women that had some of my mother's qualities and some of the other qualities that I feel that my wife will need, and some that fell way short. At the end of the day, I haven't met one that's put it all together. Maybe they feel the same about me. The bottom line is, I don't need my future wife to be perfect. I need her to be perfect for me. I need her to be a God-fearing woman that believes in God as I do and on her own, as opposed to believing what I tell her to believe. And if I can someday marry a woman with my mother's qualities, I would not only feel blessed, it would be my honor.

Chapter 2

The Un-evolution of Man

As I was writing my first book, I allowed one of my best friends to take the journey with me. Just about every word I wrote, I sent to her via email. Isn't technology wonderful? If she were an editor, I could've saved a few dollars on my publishing. As she was reading along, one of the things that she told me was that she thought that I was special in relation to other men. She felt that my views on women and life in general were so far away from the "typical male", that she just couldn't believe it sometimes. It's true, I do have a different take than my "colleagues" do on a lot of things in life, but I don't think it makes me that special. As I told her, there are guys out there like me, but it's true that we are scarce. However, I didn't want her to put me on too high of a pedestal. Most times, when that happens to us, all it means is that when we do fall, we'll have much further to go than the average person. Since I don't want that to be me, I try to remain humble.

When you're receiving that kind of praise from the opposite sex, it's sometimes hard to keep perspective. Although I like the idea of being thought of as the world's most enlightened man this side of the Mississippi, not only was I not always this way, I'm still not all the way there. I don't want to lose my status in the world of the typical male. I still like some of the same things that all of the "ordinary" men out there like. I guess what I'm saying is, although I can be sensitive at times (I mean, I do write poetry, for God's sake), I am still a man.

As I've stated once in this book, I will watch football for 11 hours straight on Sundays. I am partial to some silly movies like Mike Meyer's *Austin Powers* movies and Adam Sandler's *Eight Crazy Nights*, and I will look twice if I see a short skirt (but it has to be on the right woman; some of you need to check the mirror before leaving home). I do eat an unhealthy amount of salty snacks and sweets. I enjoy a good car chase and/or shootout in my movies. All of my colors are basic and there's no difference between eggshell, off-white and plain ol' white to me. Occasionally, I'll still do things that are convenient, as opposed to what makes sense. I don't completely understand why the toilet seat should be left down. I mean, she should look before she sits down, right? Yes ladies, it's true. Although I am more understanding than the average brotha about who you are and what you need, somewhere, deep down inside of me there still lurks a typical male.

In this chapter, I intend to give that typical male some time. I've been told by some young ladies that know me well that there are two sides to me. Well, actually they say that there are more than that, but what they mean is no matter what mood I may be in, that mood is coming from one of two people. And as ridiculous as this seems, I have named them. First, there's Kelly.

Kelly is who my mother gave birth to. Kelly is kind, gentle and understanding. Kelly is the one who'll sit up all night and be a shoulder to cry on. Kelly is the poet. Kelly sends the flowers. Kelly is who the ladies like most to deal with. In fact, I've noticed that the ladies that I've dated will always call me Kelly. Not that Kelly isn't my name, but they prefer Kelly to my alter ego.

That alter ego is KJ. For all of the things that I told you Kelly was about, KJ don't have time for any of that crap. KJ is sometimes hard to deal with. There's a certain abrasiveness to KJ. Where Kelly is honest, KJ is *brutally* honest. Where Kelly sends flowers, KJ gives you directions to the flower shop and asks you bring him something to eat when you're on your way back. However, whether it's KJ or Kelly, he's still willing to pay for it. Neither KJ nor Kelly is cheap, but KJ's just not getting out of his seat for very much. While Kelly will stay up with you all night as you cry, KJ will give you an hour or so and if he thinks you're being ridiculous, he'll tell you to get over it and go to bed.

While Kelly's the intellect and will read books that enlighten like *More Money Than God* by Rabbi Steven Leder, *Keep The Faith* by Tavis Smiley or something by Frederick Douglass, KJ likes sports, an insane amount of *The Simpsons* and those previously mentioned silly movies. While Kelly loves Prince and Miles Davis, KJ likes Jay-Z and Biggie. And Prince. While talking to Kelly in the business world, you would thinks he's from the 'burbs. But if you stick around long enough, the east side of Detroit will appear in the form of KJ.

The amusement park that is KJWorld is definitely KJ's idea because he's arrogant. He's not only gone on record as wanting his own amusement park (but unlike Neverland Ranch, there are nooooooo children allowed), he even wants his own mascot after seeing it done in a Starbucks commercial. He's the one talking to you in third person right now. In fact, from my twisted perspective, KJ's writing the first half of this book in an effort to make you laugh and bring some levity to life. But Kelly will take over in the second half in an attempt to enlighten and uplift you. Kelly's just nice that way.

Although I feel that most people have two sides like me, a lot of people don't like to admit it. As I said, KJ can be abrasive at times, but in my opinion, that's necessary sometimes. Although we have to turn the other cheek sometimes, every now and then you have to set somebody straight. All of the women that I've ever dated are aware of both sides of my personality and have used each to their advantage a time or two. However, they always hesitate when speaking KJ's name. Although they love KJ, sometimes they just don't want him showing up. He's like Beetlejuice or the Candyman. You call that name too many times and the next thing you know, he's here, all hell has broken loose and he's asking you questions like "You're not really gonna wear that, are you?" Just gotta let sleeping dogs lie sometimes.

Now that I've broken all of that down in longhand, let's get on with it. This is the man's chapter. I'll share some of my thoughts from the past, present and maybe even the future on things that most regular guys will think about from time to time. As I said in my marriage chapter, I used to have a website that only a few of my friends knew about. It was just a way for me to share my opinions on many different things. It was mostly sports, music and relationship issues, but it was my own little corner of the world. So, from what used to be my Commentary Pages, I decided to share with you some thoughts that were rolling around in my head a few years ago. We'll start with an oldie, but goodie. This was a piece I wrote on one of the greatest inventions known to man. Something near and dear to my heart. Here it is. My ode to the television remote.

Remote CONTROL!

Once again, a KJ Commentary page was born out of one simple question asked by a curious woman who just doesn't understand: "Why do men insist on being the only ones allowed to hold the remote control?" This type of relationship, no, this type of *love*, is too deep even for a woman to understand. First of all, let me dispel one myth. It has nothing to do with being an extension of our penis. That's what sports cars and power tools are for. What remotes *are* an extension of is "the gift". The gift from God. Television. To be perfectly honest, women aren't prepared to handle the remote. I apologize, ladies, but it's true. For men, this is a birthright. We are trained from the time that we are very young men to handle the remote while you girls are out playing with dolls, shopping or whatever girls do growing up. There are so many things about the remote that women just don't understand. The remote must be properly caressed. It can't be handled by just anyone. And believe me ladies, the remote knows when it's in the wrong hands. You think that it can't feel anything because it's an inanimate object, but any real man will tell you that such a thing is just not true.

Furthermore, we men know when our remotes have been mishandled and mistreated by women and children who take it, turn to a specific channel, and then leave it there. This is insanity. No remote really wants to be, well, idle like that. They need to feel loved, and the only way to do that is constant movement. Flick, flick, flick. When a commercial hits, it's time to give that remote a workout. My brother Tracey was a master at this when we were growing up. Men know that an idle remote is the devil's workshop.

I know you ladies out there believe that you're jealous of the TV. You think that the TV takes up too much of your husband's time. Why does he spend so much time with his TV? It's not the TV that's the problem, it's the remote. Men, the ladies don't like the remote because we treat it like we're supposed to treat them (at least like they *say* we're supposed to treat them). We hold it close, we caress it as I stated earlier, we treat it with love and care, we won't allow just anyone to hold and touch it, and we've even been known to fall asleep holding it tight. On the other hand ladies, we love the remote because the remote loves us. When we say "show me the goods", it does. It never needs to go shopping, it never needs us to talk to it constantly, it does exactly what we tell/program it to do, and if ever it doesn't respond, we just change the batteries. Try getting that from a woman.

Though the remote can't give you sex or food, if properly operated, it can tell where to go to get either of those things. So you see ladies, we love the remote because it represents what we want you to be: Submissive. All jokes aside ladies, the reason we're so insistent on handling the remote is because that's the only thing that a man can really control in the house. It's all about CONTROL! Of course, that's more of a problem for a married man than a single stud like me. One more perk of being single guys. There's no question who rules the remote.

Just remember ladies, we don't tell you how to max out the credit card or how to tell your friends and family "I don't know why I'm still with him", or even how to drive the car for 5 months before getting an oil change and then complain because the car is "acting weird". So don't complain about our obsession with the remote. Just sit back and enjoy the ride/channel surf with us. Enjoy the game, the gun fight, the car chase, and the naked... well, whatever we may be watching. Just give us your support. And maybe a sandwich and something to drink, please.

The comfort of the blue light

Now, before you ladies get all upset about that one, I need you to understand two things. Number one: It's just a little joke, even though there are some very true statements within the piece. Second: KJ's writing this chapter so he's not really that concerned if you're offended. If you don't like it, take it up with Kelly in the second half of the book. I took that angle in order to try and explain a man's love affair with his television to a woman. There are times in a man's life when he'd rather watch TV than do anything else in the world. Especially when sports are on. Women have often pretended not to understand this attachment. But you try and interrupt them when *America's Top Model* or *Oprah* is on. Believe me, they understand exactly what's going on.

If there's anything of a material nature that a man loves more than his car, it is his television. This is especially true if it's a large TV. If you wanna make us fall in love with something, all you have to do is make it bigger. Just think about it. Our cars became SUV's, which became full-sized SUV's (isn't that an oxymoron?), which became Hummers, for God's sake. That's right, people with no military experience felt the need to drive tanks through the city. When 12-inch subs weren't enough, we invented the *12-foot* party subs. When our fast food got too small, we super *and* biggie sized it. When storefronts weren't enough, we built a mall (that actually worked out for the ladies). When the c-cup wasn't enough, we came up with breast implants. And when our stadiums became too small, we made them all bigger, which made the live action game much further away from the cheap seats.

However, not to be defeated, we came up with the Jumbo Tron, our giant TV at the game, conveniently located in the middle of the scoreboard so that we don't have to look in too many directions to get all of our information. We can check the score, watch instant replays, see which celebrities may be at the game and watch all kinds of idiots make asses of themselves once the realize they're on the big screen.

With all of that said, it was just a matter of time before we felt that we had to create TV's that rivaled drive-in screens. We started out by creating small, portable televisions that we could take anywhere in case we wound up in a place where we didn't wanna pay attention. In that unfortunate event, we could always count on the flickering blue light and the little people on the screen to take us away. Even worse, how often have you seen a guy at a sporting event with a portable TV, watching the very game that he's attending? His reasoning? He wants to hear what the announcers are saying about the game or he wants to see the network replays as opposed to just seeing the arena replays. Just staying home was not an option.

From there, we decided that if we could make them small and portable, why not make them large and gargantuan? Why not make the television experience at home more enjoyable? First, we decided to change the programming and came up with things like affordable satellite service, ESPN, The NFL Network, NBA League Pass, NFL Sunday Ticket, and so on and so forth. Man was in his glory, but there was still something missing. We have to bring all of these wonderful things into our homes in a larger and more fantastic way. Why not make the TV's larger? After all, bigger is always better. So we did, and now you can hardly tear us away. We've even taken over our children's Playstations and X-BOXs so that we can play video games on a larger scale. We've even been known to only consider buying houses with basements large enough to accommodate our large screened addictions.

If you're a woman that can't understand why your man has to have such a big TV, you should know that we have that same lack of understanding about you and your engagement ring. You wanna know why we can't just get a reasonable sized TV that's basically showing us the same thing as the big screen, and we wanna know why you can't just take a reasonably sized ring if our love for you is basically the same. Neither is really a necessity, but we've both convinced ourselves that these are the things we need to be happy. The thing is, a man has great reverence for his TV. We allow it to tell us what to think, how to feel, what the standard of beauty is in a woman (although, women are guilty of that, too), what teams to root for, what to buy, what to drink, and even what to do when time catches up with us and we're either bald, impotent or both. We're even willing to let it raise our children when the wife isn't watching.

At the end of the day, above all, a man's TV is the equivalent of a baby's pacifier. We haven't really changed a lot since we were kids and our parents used to sit us down in front of the TV just to keep us occupied while they took some very important "me time". Or better yet, TV is a man's drug. It's so far out of control, that we need rehab. They moved from the living room, to the palms of our hands, to the basement (in some cases, covering walls completely), and eventually, to our cars, trucks and vans. They're even in the cell phones, for God's sake.

How do I know all of these things? I'm an addict, that's how. Who'd be better qualified to spot an addict than another addict? That's what makes the remote so powerful. How many addicts can control their drug from across the room? Instead of rebelling, women should take the role of parent or drug dealer. If you wanna settle your child or your junkie down and stop them from complaining about whatever or harassing you for sex, just sit them down in front of the TV and they're sure to settle into a nice football game and give you the time and space that you need. Remember, "it's science".

Please, don't make me waste $10

Greater than the divide that separates men and women in the TV world, is the divide that separates us in the movie world. If you think that we have trouble agreeing on what and how much TV to watch, it's even worse when we're trying to choose a movie that all will enjoy. I want *Die Hard*, she wants *Pretty Woman*. I want *Lethal Weapon*, she wants *Love Jones*. I want *Austin Powers*, she wants *How Stella Got Her Groove Back*. It goes on and on. For me, the only thing harder than finding someone that shares my taste in cinema, is finding someone that shares my taste in music.

Don't get me wrong, I'm not all action movies and shootouts. I tend to like movies with great dialogue and intellect as well. Movies with a message are also good for me. But if it don't get romantic at some point for the ladies, I'm usually up a creek.

With all of this division between man and woman on what movies to go see, it caused me to wonder how much money is wasted by forcing men to watch movies that they could care less about, or women choosing to watch movies that they're horrified by, all in the name of spending time with their "boo". I mean, couldn't this money be used in a more practical way? Gas for the car? Charity? A good sandwich? A bargain bin DVD from Best Buy? The possibilities are endless.

I know that couples these days couldn't bear to do things without one another. Perish the thought. However, shouldn't we at least consider it? Women go to dinner together all the time, why not dinner and a lame movie? Now, I'm not suggesting that all of the love stories that women are into are lame. Well, maybe I am. I'm not really sure. But the point is, if a woman has an interest in a love story, movies that make them cry or a "chick flick", chances are, her best friend is into that same movie. Don't force a man to suffer through such things if he doesn't want to. Take a friend. It's what's best for all.

Now, a woman reading this may wonder why she has to suffer through Sunday after Sunday of NFL action (doesn't it just sound wonderful guys?), if her man can't suffer through 2 ½ hours of on screen indecision from Julia Roberts about whether she wants to marry one snobbish white man or another. Well, the answers are obvious. First, there's probably another TV in the house that she can go and watch while we men are in the trenches. However, there's no way that we can change the channel on the screen at the theater. Sure, there are other movies playing in the theater, but are you ladies gonna let us get away with going to see another movie when we rode together? I think not.

Second, it's very simple. It's a double standard, duh! We don't really care about your being angry about our hours of football watching. The ability to watch all of those games is worth you being angry. I wish it weren't true ladies, but it is. As silly as it sounds, we'll trade your happiness for the opportunity to watch other men for several hours any day of the week. We already know that no matter how angry you get, it's nothing that a dozen roses and a pair of shoes can't fix. Well, at least I know that.

Now, don't get angry with what I'm saying ladies. Remember, it's just my sense of humor. I'm just trying to write a funny book and in the course of doing that, I may give a few funny anecdotes and tell a few jokes. I mean, honestly, I'm not going anywhere near a women's shoe store and roses are for special occasions only. Wow, maybe it's just me, but I could've sworn I just heard several of my books slamming shut in disgust. Kelly hopes that you'll forgive as women are prone to doing and come back later and finish the book. KJ is indifferent about the whole thing.

The brains of the operation

Getting back to the "science" that I've referenced a few times in this book, you remember that I took it from the movie *Anchorman: The Legend of Ron Burgundy*. During the scene that I referenced, Ron was suggesting that it was "science" that determined that men were smarter than women. I don't know what's funnier, that scene or the fact that a lot of men actually believe that. Ron suggested that because he was "a man that invented the wheel and built the Eiffel Tower out of metal and brawn", that he was, therefore, smarter than any woman could ever be. It's weird how some things can make you laugh because they're accurate.

In the comedic senselessness of Will Ferrell, he was holding a mirror up to men all around the world. No matter how enlightened some men may be, the majority of us think that we're smarter than women. And if you really break it down, it's mostly because we're physically stronger and because throughout history, we've invented and built more things than women have. Even KJ's not arrogant enough to believe that, but it does make me wonder why such perceptions exist.

I was a young man when I realized that women were more knowledgeable than men. So many times when we get into the "who's smarter" debate, we always go straight to book sense, but something like that is completely subjective anyway. That can't be broken down into gender as far as I'm concerned. For example, one of my younger nieces had higher grade point average than her older sister during one card marking. They got into a little bit of an argument because the older one said to the younger one, "You think you're smarter than me, but you ain't" (that certainly raised one of my eyebrows). The younger one responded by saying, "I'm not smarter than you, I just work harder". Touché little sista, touché.

The better student is usually the one that works the hardest. It's just as simple as that. The reasons that women are smarter than men go beyond just intellect. Strangely enough, it's because they're in touch with their feelings. Yeah, I made fun of them a few lines back for crying at movies, but that's what makes them better off than we are. The fact that they hold nothing back emotionally for the most part, keeps them from sinking to our levels. Because we build and we're strong and we're the head of this company and that team, we instantly think we're smarter. But if you've ever had an idiot boss, you already know that you don't have to be particularly smart to be in charge of anything.

All you have to do is look at who was running the country for those 8 pre-Obama years.

It's been said that it's a man's world, and that's very true in most ways. Although that doesn't explain why we should be in charge, it does explain why so much is screwed up so often. We only think in terms of what we can physically see. The only emotion we're comfortable showing outwardly is anger. Second to that is jealousy, which may as well be the cousin of anger. We hesitate to show love. We hesitate to show affection. We hesitate to cry. But we've invented things like road rage and the riot. Trust me, these things were not brought about by women.

It's true, women can be too soft sometimes, but that's what makes them women. That's what we like about them (or, at least I do). Sometimes, they can be too tolerant, and we as men mock them for that. However, we never mocked that quality in a woman when we were young and it was your mom and she was trying to keep from killing you because you broke her favorite vase or you broke curfew. Or when it's your woman and she's trying to keep from leaving you because you insist on cheating (we'll get to that momentarily).

Although it may seem very complicated to explain, to me, it's really just that simple. Because we tend to be unbalanced emotionally, women are usually just better off than we are. They know how to let things out. They know how to love. They know how to be affectionate. They know how to cry. And, most importantly, they know how to forgive. They won't forget, but they will forgive. On the other hand, men will forget more than they forgive. But if you remind us why we were mad in the first place, we're pissed all over again. Because we're so "tough" and women are so "soft", this leads men to thinking that we're somehow smarter, when all we really are is tougher. There is something that can be said about the toughness of man, but without that other side, we are unbalanced. Without that other side, we carry around a lot of unnecessary emotion that usually manifests itself at the worst times.

Because most women will release that, they usually don't carry around the tensions that men do. There are some bag ladies out there that will carry a lot of things around with them, but women will usually exhale at some point. Women are unbalanced as well and will tend to be *too* emotional and wear their emotions on their sleeves too often, but that's actually better than the alternative of holding it all in as we do. The general thought is that women aren't tough because they tend to be a little soft, but how do you explain their ability to put up with us? When you consider that we will make them cry quite often, how do you explain them coming back to us time after time? If that ain't tough, I don't know what is. We want to believe that women can't run anything because they can be too emotional. What we must realize is that a little emotion is what's needed sometimes.

When pointing to the fact that women aren't in charge of very much in a worldly sense, and therefore aren't smarter than men, all you have to do is look at history to dispel that myth. When were they ever allowed to be in charge of anything? We never knew they were capable of anything besides reproduction because we spent so much time suppressing them. That's why I said in my chapter on marriage that women should seek to establish themselves as individuals before they sought so quickly to attach themselves to some man. The opportunity is there in today's world, you may as well take advantage of it. They have the same ability to be CEO's, inventers, Governors, Mayors or whatever they want to be. And on top of all of that, they have the natural ability to be nurturers and mothers. How real is that? Sorry fellas, they're ahead of the game, even though some of them don't know it or refuse to assert themselves.

Can a man be smarter than a woman? Of course he can, especially if he's like me and he already knows what he's up against. Am I smarter than woman? I'm smarter than a lot of them, but I've met many that were smarter than I am. I believe I can hold my own with them. That much I do know. Why? Because I treat it like a sport and I respect my opponent. A woman has to prove to me that she *isn't* intelligent before I'll just believe it.

Upon first meeting a woman, I don't believe that I can have a thought that she's not capable of having herself. It's only when she proves to be less enlightened that I believe that I have a mental edge on a woman. Do I then take advantage of that? Contrary to popular belief, I don't. If she stays near me, I would hope to enlighten her, just as the many, many intelligent women that I've known throughout my life have enlightened me. That's one more thing that men must understand. When you have knowledge, you should share knowledge, as opposed to keeping it to yourself in fear that if you enlighten her, she'll overtake you. If she seeks to overtake you, there's nothing you can do to stop her from trying anyway. At that point, it's just a part of her nature.

And speaking of things that are a part of a person's nature, how smart do you think we are when you consider the fact that we're so horrible at cheating? Don't get me wrong, women seem to cheat as much as we do these days, but if you're a man that wants to cheat, why not ask a woman how to do it? This is an old adage and I'm not telling you anything that you haven't heard before, but it's always amazed me that we sometimes don't realize that they are better at this than we are. Why? Well, to know why they're better is to know why they're doing it.

Again, it goes back to the emotion of it. Now, this is something that I covered lightly in my first book, and in my poetry book in a piece called "The Glass". And again, unfortunately, I have to preference all that I'm saying by letting you know that I'm talking about women that don't usually do this kind of thing. The ones that are frequent cheaters are just as sloppy as men are, so they get caught about as much as men do. And just like men, they don't seem to get why they shouldn't do what they do until they're actually caught doing it.

As I said, the reason that a faithful woman winds up cheating is because of the emotion of it. A faithful woman is so wrapped up in her current situation, that the last thing she wants to do is cheat. She loves her man so much that even if he's treating her wrong, not spending time with her, or cheating himself, she wants to try to work it out rather than get even. However, sometimes that idiot man will push her so far that she loses her composure and she retaliates. But unlike a cheating man, that woman isn't reactionary.

The faithful woman isn't going to do something just because she supposedly can or because she has nothing else to occupy her mind. She's only going to do it when she's been severely hurt, has had enough and she needs to feel some measure of satisfaction through revenge. But because she's still in love, has invested so much of herself into the relationship and still doesn't want to leave this knucklehead, she's going to put some thought into what she's going to do.

She's not gonna grab the first dude willing to help her cause. She's not gonna grab some dude from work that's been hounding

44

her for the last six months, so it can spread through the office like wildfire, ruin her reputation and then her significant other finds out when this loser gets drunk at the Christmas party. I've actually dated three women in my past that fell victim to that scenario, minus the Christmas party. As I said, if you get sloppy, you get caught and some loser is at the copy machine the next morning spreading the fact that he spread your legs to all who'll listen. This won't happen to the faithful and enlightened woman. Her choice is gonna be so well thought out and so cleverly planned, that even the man she chooses will be caught off guard. And you wanna know the kicker, fellas? You'll never find out unless she wants you to.

The consolation prize for men in all of this is the fact that our women didn't become such geniuses at this on their own. We were their source of enlightenment on this one. They learned what they learned about cheating from us and our cheating ways. But in the way that women do a lot of things, they took what we did, analyzed it, figured out our flaws, and damn near perfected what we thought was our craft. We were so "smart", that we thought that every time they caught us cheating, they cried, yelled and screamed, and when they'd had enough, packed up their emotions and moved on. But as I told you earlier, they forgive, but they don't forget. Every time we teach them a new "trick", they put it away in a glass case and they break it on the next man in case of emergency. They never forget how they caught you and they never forget what your behavior was leading up to her catching you. So from there, they not only know what to look for in the next man, they know how not to be when they're getting ready to do their dirt.

Again, this is all in reference to the faithful and enlightened woman out there. This is the woman that wants to stand by her man, but he just won't do right and he's making her wonder if he's worth the trouble. This is the woman that wants to have her man's back, but he keeps coming home smelling like other women. This is the woman that's looking to keep the family together, but her man can't accept another woman flirting with him with gentle good humor without trying to oblige her by getting her number and taking it further than it has to go.

If we were less reactionary and more thoughtful, less abrasive and more caring, less intolerant and more tolerant, we might have a shot at the all-time smarter than thou title. However, we're so convinced that if we show any emotion other than anger and outrage, that it's a sign of weakness. In one sense, we have to maintain some of our hard exterior. Just like some of those softer qualities are what makes a woman a woman, these harder qualities make a man a man, and women appreciate that. But sometimes, we have to be willing to let some of that hard exterior take a back seat. No woman wants a soft man, but a compassionate one is okay. Believe it or not, it's that side of you, along with the ability to cry when you hurt, that shows your real strength. I like to tell a joke from time to time that the only time its okay for a man to cry is when someone dies or when his team loses. I realize it's a joke, but I could swear I just heard some man grunt "Amen!"

I'd like to speak to someone in charge...

If there's ever been an argument that's waged longer than who's smarter between men and women, it has to be, who's really the boss. Well, as with anything else, it depends on which gender you actually ask, and what we're talking about. There are times when it benefits a man to be in charge, but there are also times when a woman should take the lead. In most cases, she's the boss. However, women have a way of making us think that we're in charge. From what I've observed from the married couples that I've known, the wife lets the husband *think* he's in charge, when in fact, she's running the show. It's really like some Jedi mind trick that she works on him. She lets him lead as long as he goes where she tells him to go. But as long as a man's in the front of the line, he's in charge as far as he's concerned.

I have a friend that's married and I once asked him, "Who's the boss in your house?" He told me in no uncertain terms, "I'm the man of my house". He still remains unaware that he never answered my question. Considering the fact that he and his wife still have no children, being the man of the house is no great accomplishment. I mean, who else is going to be the man of the house, his wife? Again, another mind trick.

A wife will always tell her husband that he's the man of the house in an attempt to make him feel important. But, think about it men, what does man of the house really mean? I'll tell you what it means. If it breaks, you fix it. If she buys it, you build it. If you build it wrong, you listen to her complain, and then you rebuild it. If it's overflowing, you take it out. If it's small and furry and runs really fast, you kill it and get rid of it. If it's overflowing with junk that *she* refuses to throw away, when she grows weary of it, you clean it out. If the pets die, you tell the kids. And last, but certainly not least, if they break into the house bearing arms, looking to take all that we own, you go downstairs and take the first bullet. Why? Because you're the man of the house.

What all of this means is that you may be the king of your particular castle, but you're probably not in charge of a damn thing. What I told my friend was that he may be the "man of the house", but his wife was in charge. He didn't seem to think so, but I solved it all with two questions. Question one: How often do you make purchases without your wife's knowledge? And for my follow up, I asked, how often does she make them without your knowledge? Game, set and match to KJ. Now, I hate to keep coming back to this, but I'm speaking about the good ones, not those "less than" women that some of us will marry. Because we can think no further than the nose on our faces, most men can't run the household the way it needs to be run. The wife will go out and buy things all the time without the husband's knowledge because even if it's frivolous, she does it within the framework of the household budget. Translation: She'll budget for her wants, but she'll only budget for your needs.

Why is that, you say? Because a man's frivolous purchases are spontaneous in nature. They usually only make sense to us and we want to make them at the worst times, at the expense of any bill. Like a large, flat screen TV when junior's tuition is due. However, though a woman's frivolous purchases may *seem* spontaneous, they are usually planned. Now, a lot of women may think that their new pair of shoes was spontaneous, but in reality, it was subconsciously planned. Most women won't go to the mall, the shoe store, Wal-Mart or wherever without at least the anticipation of buying something. Because she sometimes doesn't know what she's going to buy, even she thinks the purchase is spontaneous. But it's not.

In this case, she Jedi mind tricks herself and she makes the purchase, all the while believing that she's living in the "danger zone" and doing something so unexpected. The fact is, if a woman's in the vicinity of any store, I expect money to be spent. Think about it, guys. Haven't you ever noticed that whenever you want to buy something outrageous, it's "not the right time" or "we can't afford that now"? But as soon as there's a super sale somewhere, she comes home loaded down with inventory, and then has the nerve to ask you to help her get it out of the car. If you don't know who the boss is, I weep for your deteriorating mental health.

In the end, to me, it's all good. I've often stated that I won't marry a woman unless she can run the household. I'm willing to go to work and bring home the bacon if she'd simply take care of all of the things that I just don't feel like taking care of. She can budget the money and include that new pair of shoes all she wants, as long as she gets all of the important things done, like the satellite bill. My ex-girlfriend created this monster as she spoiled the hell out of me. I'll be the man of the house, and she can be the boss. I'll be in my glory when we take family vacations and I get to drive. I won't need any directions from her because unlike most men, I've never been lost no matter what city I've been in.

There are certain things that a good wife is capable of that most men just aren't. I asked my friend, as he tried feverously to convince me that he carried some weight in his home, "When is it time to buy more toilet paper?" "When you know you're running out", he answered smugly. Idiot. He doesn't know any better because he never had to do that for himself. He answered like a bachelor would answer. Ask that of a man that's been married to a good woman for 5 years or more and he won't have an answer. Why? Because he doesn't deal in toilet paper unless he's on the toilet. And because he's got a good woman, he never has to answer that question because the toilet paper is always there. It's really more because of her than him when you consider that she needs it on every trip, but now we're getting into semantics. The bottom line is, worse case scenario, someone has to bring it to the bathroom from the linen closet, but no one has to run to the store while you're held hostage on a porcelain throne.

Now, I'm not suggesting that men can't learn to be domesticated. If you're a bachelor and you were raised by the type of woman that I was raised by, you have no choice. You're domesticated when you leave mama's house. But we all long to get back to the days when all we have to do is be the "man of the house". Women have a natural instinct when it comes to taking care of home that men just aren't born with. There are plenty of single dads out there that do a great job, but we have a lot more to learn our first time out than women do. Because they have that natural ability to love, care and show the compassion that I spoke of earlier, they're already ahead of us, even with their first experiences with children.

Again, the adage is old, but they're natural caretakers, and we're natural hunters. We can kill it and bring it home, but it takes mama to cook it and properly proportion it so that her family can not only be fed for the evening, but fed for days to come. We as men all long for the days when we feel like we're back at home with mama. I can handle that trash. I can build that entertainment center. Small and furry? Consider him terminated. Just keep me out of Wal-Mart.

Chapter 3

"Friends, lovers and otherwise..."

A sure sign that one is getting older is when you start to notice that times have changed. Phrases like "when I was comin' up..." or "I remember a time when..." start to become a regular part of your speech. You remember when certain buildings were built *and* torn down. Your favorite car has gone through 2 or 3 different changes in body style. More importantly, you notice that things in general aren't done the way they used to be. Everything from customer service at your favorite restaurant to etiquette and manners seem to have taken a different turn these days.

Something I remember is how important a man's word used to be. I mean, there was a time when a man's word was the measure of him. In a lot of ways, it was all he had. He was only as good as his word. So it was always imperative that he keep it. The last thing you wanted was for someone to see you as a person that couldn't keep his word. If you were labeled that way, you were a half step from being a liar. I say only a half step because sometimes there are circumstances that will keep us from keeping our word. So some people that can't keep their word aren't necessarily liars. A bit unreliable, but not necessarily liars. So what's happened to us over the years? Why doesn't anybody want to keep their word anymore?

As the title of this chapter suggests, this isn't just a problem with a friend or a lover. It's a problem everywhere. The general assumption is that one has to actually tell a lie in order to be thought of as a person that can't keep their word. But if you violate a trust, violate a relationship or violate wedding vows that you took before God, you've broken your word. And depending on how severe that violation was, you can be thought of as a liar and one that can't keep their word.

In addition to that, we don't value the love that we supposedly share anymore. It's become secondary to so many other things, namely money and the pursuit thereof and the unwillingness to sacrifice for the well-being of the relationship. Things that used to be the fabric of any relationship or true friendship are no longer of any importance anymore. "I remember a time when we didn't do things like this". Life mattered, love mattered, honesty mattered and friendships mattered. I'm left to wonder, has my time come and gone?

Who wants to be a millionaire?

I recently asked a bunch of people that I know if they still believed in love. I didn't ask it quite so bluntly, but I asked them how their lives were different based on whether or not they were in love. Do the flowers still smell the same? Does your life seem better? Are you more willing to get up every morning? In general, do you just feel better when you're in love as opposed to when you're not? The answers I got were quite surprising.

I'll start by telling you how I feel. Life is always better when you're in love. Your problems don't seem as severe. Life's ups and downs are a lot easier to handle. Trouble on your job doesn't bother you as much. And yes, the flowers do smell better to me when I'm in love. I guess I qualify as a hopeless romantic, but it seems to me that life would always be better if you had someone in your life that loved you.

What I found out was that very few shared that sentiment, including one particular individual I had been involved with. She said to me that it didn't really affect her either way and that her life was the same whether she was in love or not. I guess that's why we never worked out. When you feel the love in a relationship, you feel the pain when you're losing it. Most times, when you're aware that you have love, you'll work hard to maintain it. I'm also noticing that with the decrease of a love that makes a day-to-day difference in one's life comes the decrease in one's willingness to save that love if it seems to be leaving. Because we see our lives the same either way, we can't see the importance in holding on. We have become jaded about love.

Let me give you an example. Say you had a job that paid you a million dollars a year. I'm sure that those of us that don't already have that good fortune would love to be in that position. Now, say after six months on the job, your boss came to you and told you that you weren't performing up to expectations. Say he told you that he needed more out of you or he'd have to replace you. Now, at the same time, say you felt that you were giving all that you could to the company. You were working late nights, coming in on weekends and all that. Sure, sometimes you didn't give 100% and there were days when you just gave a half effort while collecting a whole paycheck, but for the most part, you were faithful and got the job done as far as you could tell. In this situation, what would you do?

How many of you said that you would just quit? Not very many of you, I'm sure. For those that did initially say that they would quit, I want you to really think before you answer. A million dollar a year job. Those aren't just lying around these days. Considering that you were giving your all, or at the very least a lot, most of us would initially be pissed. I mean, yeah, you're getting paid a million dollars and all, and sometimes you don't work as hard as you should, but you still get the job done. Why is the boss coming down on you so hard? That's how most of us would react. But after we calmed ourselves, we'd go back to work, tighten up where we should and recommit ourselves to making the job work. After all, this is a million dollar a year job. My question is this: Why don't we treat our relationships the same way?

I feel that I've suffered as much as anyone at the hands of people who either didn't love me like they said they did or just don't take love as seriously as I do. And people wonder why I can't marry in this climate? Anyway, the love that you share with another has to be worth your time, energy and effort. Life's too short to just be going through the motions. In the example that I used in the last few paragraphs, it's evident where some of our priorities are. We tend to place more faith in what we can see as opposed to what we feel. That's why some of us can't follow God, no matter what God you serve. It requires faith and we're more willing to believe in what we see.

That million dollar job can pay the bills. That million dollar job can pay for nice cars and nice vacations. It can buy good looking clothes and provide financial security. All love can do is make sure that you're paying the bills of someone that matters, buying cars for someone that means the world to you, clothing the love of your life or making sure that if you go on that expensive vacation, you'll have a great time because who you go with is most times more important than where you go. That's all that love can do for you. But we'd rather tell someone that we make a million dollars a year than tell someone that we're in love and we couldn't be happier.

This all goes back to man's belief that money can buy happiness. But all you have to do is look at the entertainment industry that we so praise and see how many miserable people you see. All of their problems manifest themselves in the form of drug abuse, illegal behavior, infidelity or feelings of emptiness. It's an old saying, but all that glitters ain't gold. We don't place a premium on love anymore. Sure, one day I'd like to be financially secure enough to not have to worry about how I'm going to pay any bill. But I can assure you that all that I amass in life will be that much sweeter if I have the love of a good woman to share it with. Conversely, whether I reach millionaire status or not, I'm sure that there are struggles regardless. Having that love in your life will always help to ease the pain and lift the weight.

I know that in these tough economical times, money's importance has been increased. But it never has and never will be more important than love. It can't keep you warm the way a loved one can, it can't hold you when you need to be held, it can't comfort you when you need to be comforted and when you want to hear those three words it will remain silent. If money is all that you have and all that you're about, then it's more likely to cause problems than solve them. Your relationship must be built on a strong foundation of trust and respect if it is to survive. Without that, you can have as many millions as you'd like, but you'll still make a fool of yourself at some point. Read on...

"He shoots, he scores...but there's a foul on the play..."

Did you guys hear that one thing about Kobe Bryant a few years ago? About the white girl? Eagle, Colorado? Cheatin' on the wife? 19 year old hotel hook–, I mean, worker? Unless you were in a comatose state or living under a rock, of course you did. This July 2003 case shocked the entire world. Not just the NBA world, not just the sports world, but the entire world. If we had seen it coming, we all would've ducked. But because we didn't, we were all sucker punched right in the mouth. How could our African-American dream and heir-apparent to the Michael Jordan throne get caught up like that?

I still remember when word was beginning to leak out that young Kobe might have run afoul of the law. I'm thinking maybe an unpaid parking ticket, somebody forgot to pay the bar tab or maybe even a little possession of the chronic. Hell, maybe even a DUI. I mean, he is a NBA player. I think DUI allowance is probably part of the collective bargaining agreement. I figured this was much ado about nothing. I figured Kobe got caught up in the thin air of Eagle, CO. and lost his head. Forgot about his skin color and ran a red light or something. Just a little misunderstanding between rich folks. Well, it was a misunderstanding, alright.

As news continued to come out, the words "sexual" and "assault" began to find themselves next to one another rather frequently. It was beginning to look worse and worse for Brandy's former prom date. But it was still so hard to believe. I mean, this was Kobe frickin' Bryant. A 'hood hero, even though he was a little bourgeois. This was the man our kids were looking up to. This was the man that had that winning smile that Jordan and Magic Johnson before him possessed. In the wake of Kobe's legendary promise, the 'hood had finally come to grips with Michael's retirement. Oh, but we had no idea of the dark side that existed behind that smile.

Okay, let's cover what we already knew. Kobe has a thing for young, white girls. We knew that when he started dating his eventual wife while she was still in high school. When we came to grips with the fact that our hero had allegedly sexually assaulted someone, the fact that she was a young, white girl should have been a surprise to no one. I mean, me and some of the brothas, and definitely some of the sistas, had *hoped* that Kobe would stay to the darker side. That trip to the prom with the previously mentioned Brandy gave us hope. Unfortunately, that truly was a publicity stunt. Kobe likes his coffee with lots and lots of cream.

From the beginning, I said that I didn't think there was an assault. I felt all along that Kobe simply got caught with his, uh, pants down. No matter what the Colorado prosecutor's office may want you to believe, they agree with me too. There's no way they let the brotha walk free if they have enough evidence to convict. But the closer we came to trial, the more we learned about his accuser. The wild ways that her parents probably already knew about, but turned a blind eye to. The fact that after her examination following the alleged rape, there was allegedly semen from three different men, including Bryant. With all of these things circulating, there was no sure way of getting a conviction, and in the eyes of White America, they were staring a smaller scale O.J. trial in the face.

And it didn't really matter to me what color his wife was, he was married with a child. He had no business with another woman. If you can't keep it locked up, then maybe you shouldn't get married. Even before the tearful apology and admission of infidelity on national television (with wife by his side protecting her investment), I believed that the only thing Kobe was guilty of was being stupid. Eagle, CO. already hates that fact that you could probably buy and sell everyone in their little town, and you go up there and do one of their daughters? That's one lane you shouldn't be driving.

But a disagreement in the bedroom doesn't always constitute sexual assault. That's what I think we saw. She gave Kobe a list of five things she was willing to do. Being a modern day athlete suffering from the disease of entitlement, the brotha went for six. To quote The Beatles, "you say 'goodbye', and I say 'hello'". It's semantics, but not sexual assault. You try that with your wife, you may have to pay for it with a new outfit, a pair of shoes and possibly even a $4 million dollar ring (what Kobe reportedly bought his wife as an apology gift; I may have just had to give her a heartfelt "my bad"). But if I may use another quote, this time from Ray Liotta as Henry Hill in the movie *Goodfellas*, "Nobody goes to jail, Karen".

When this case was going on, we got to thinking here in KJWorld. Why hasn't this kind of thing happened more often? Now mind you, this isn't the first time that a black professional athlete has been accused of inappropriate behavior with the ladies. I mean, let's not forget Mike Tyson. But all of this news coverage over a little infidelity? I mean, really. Isn't a famous athlete/

entertainer and his groupies a given? Isn't complaining about these things so old-fashioned? Shouldn't we get over ourselves and stay out of Kobe's business? Maybe, but I still had to wonder, how could Kobe have "gotten away" with this, and what if Kobe's accuser had been a regular, around the way girl from the 'hood?

Sad to say, if Kobe had gotten out of hand with "Shaniqua", this would've been a non-issue. A 19 year old black girl in this position would've handled this completely different. Now before my brothas and sistas get upset with me, let's examine the situation carefully. Let's look at all of the particulars. We have a girl that's loose and parents that don't care enough to be concerned. This case proved that blacks haven't cornered the market on such behavior, but we must remember that it is a problem that's too prevalent with us. The difference is that if we had a black mother with the same shortcomings as this girl's mother in this situation, and she found out her daughter had been "assaulted" by Kobe, they probably would've hi-fived each other. And then they would've gotten Kobe on the phone to see how much he was willing to do to keep this quiet.

You think I'm lying? You think I'm perpetuating stereotypes about our black women? You have no idea how many sistas, old and young, that I put this question to before I wrote these pages. I was disturbed and saddened to find that so many of them said they would've never said a word to anybody as long as Kobe "took care of a few things for them". Even Kobe thought that's how it was supposed to go. He said so when the cops were interviewing him after he was arrested/turned himself in. He said that other NBA players had told him that this kind of thing happened all of the time and all he had to do was take care of his hoochie with a few tickets to games, the occasional all expenses paid trip to, say, an All-Star game (so that either the affair can continue or she could have her shot at all of the ballers), and a few gifts here and there. What the naïve Kobe didn't understand was that you couldn't just do this with any ol' woman. There's a groupie code of "ethics" that must be adhered to. There was a groupie directory somewhere of women that were willing to play along.

What Kobe didn't understand was that he couldn't do this with a young, white woman that already had considerable wealth. You had to prey on women, whether white or black, with low self esteem that were looking to score a sexual encounter with a world famous athlete. Most 19 year old white women with that kind of money aren't quite opportunistic yet. They're already having their needs met by parents that would rather spoil them and make them think that the world owes them something because they're rich, rather than teach them morals. This young lady was still in mall mode. I'm sure her mind was kinda like "Oh my GOD, Jenny, I can't believe it, it's Kobe Bryant!!!!" She probably wanted him to sign her jeans, take a picture with her on her camera phone and maybe give her a kiss. But Kobe's a grown man, a la Mike Tyson. If you come to his hotel room, it's on, and you should know that. I think we all do now.

Kobe didn't understand that rich white folks not only have the police on speed dial, they get right through to the Chief of Police, especially in a small town like that. Rich white folks have perceptions of their children that often aren't true. The have a sense that their money buys them immunity from the ills that the rest of us face. They think that this type of thing could never happen to their children. Their children could never wind up on drugs, on the wrong side of the law or on some sex tape circulating on the internet (right Paris?). So when this type of thing shows up at their front door, they want heads to roll, whether their child is embarrassed and ashamed or not, and especially if it's at the hands of a black man. Even if it is Kobe Bryant. They'll cheer all day and all night for him, but if he even *allegedly* violates one of their daughters, they want him under the jail. Never mind their daughters, *they* have images to protect.

<u>So, we're just gonna pretend that didn't happen, right?</u>

Cheating is something that I touched on in my first book, *Temporarily Disconnected*. In my opinion, the biggest mistake made in relationships as it pertains to cheating is pretending that we never saw the signs. They're always there, but we like to sit back and pretend that they weren't. We tell ourselves that if we don't see the cheating with our own two eyes, then we can't believe what all of the evidence seems to suggest. Even though our mates can't answer the simplest questions like "Where were you?" or "Who were you with?", we tend not to believe what we can clearly see is going on. What your head and common sense is telling you, your heart simply refuses to accept. But if you're a stable and level headed person, you sometimes have to trust your head when it comes to matters of the heart.

In relation to the Kobe Bryant situation, this is what his wife should have known. She shouldn't have suspected that her husband would cheat simply because he's a professional athlete, as I'm sure some of you are thinking. If she felt that way before the nuptials, she should have never married him, no matter what his status was. His money and fame doesn't grant him immunity from the responsibilities of marriage. He has a responsibility to his wife and children to be faithful and tattooing their names on his arm and expensive jewelry won't ease the pain. If anything, the ring or the "I'm sorry" gift only serves as a constant reminder of what you've done wrong, so maybe it's not such a good thing after all. In conjunction with all of that, we as a people need to stop telling ourselves that being faithful is unrealistic and old-fashioned. If you accept less than all from your partner, they will surely give you less than all.

Kobe is still just a man and I'm sure the same signs that a cheater displays were there. I'm not sure that his wife turned a blind eye to some things. She more than likely turned a naïve eye to some things because she was so young and not ready for marriage. I have a hard time believing that this was the first time Kobe cheated and it may not have been the first time she found out. This was just the first time that the whole world found out. So something had to be done. Call the jeweler.

In so many ways, we have no idea how to treat one another when in a relationship, committed or otherwise. All of the respect seems to be gone. For example, what do you do when something inappropriate happens in your relationship? A phone call in the middle of the night from an alleged "friend" of the opposite sex when you're lying next to your partner. An unannounced visit from that same friend when your partner is there beside you. Whether you're doing it or having it done to you, when something inappropriate happens, it should be addressed. So many times, we ignore it. We may shoot a look at someone, raise an eyebrow or let out a sigh to show our displeasure and let that person know how we feel, but is that really addressing what happened? No, not really. Our hope is that the offending party saw or heard our reaction, read it correctly and will act accordingly to make sure such a thing never happens again. In the mind of one in love, those signs mean "don't let it happen again". In the mind of the offending person it simply means "fine tune your game so that we don't have to see that look or hear that sigh again".

If you don't demand an explanation for what happened in front of you, it will happen again and again, each time with a better and more prepared excuse. If I had a girlfriend and she and I were together and someone that was supposed to be just a friend rung my phone at 3am or just decided to drop by without legitimate reasoning, the next time I spoke with that person, they might not ever call again. When you're in a relationship or even when you're trying to start one, there are some things that your friends should understand and respect. All real emergencies aside, appearances can tear a relationship apart. If you have a friend that doesn't respect the fact that they shouldn't call you after a certain hour unless it's an actual emergency, whether you're in a relationship or not, then you have to re-evaluate what type of friend you're dealing with.

Now for some of you cheaters and liars out there, this isn't an excuse to tell your partner that it's an emergency every time that phone rings when it shouldn't. I know that's where some of you were headed and that's what some of you already do. How do I know? I don't claim to have lived a perfect life. I've told that lie a few times before myself. But the truth of the matter is if you have a "friend" that's making that call too often, then *you* are the emergency. "What are you doing?" "Where are you?" "Is she/he there with you?" I'm sure we all know what I'm talking about.

It all comes back to respect for your relationship and your partner. I've been in this situation before. I was with someone that claimed she loved me and her cell phone not only started ringing at 1am, it was blowing up so bad I almost offered to drive her to him for fear that he may be getting ready jump off a bridge or something. The worst part about it was she would have never said a word about it. She looked at the phone the first time to see who it was, she didn't seem surprised and she continued on watching TV with me as if nothing was going on. Every 2 minutes, her phone vibrating. Every 2 minutes, I'm expecting and explanation or an apology. Every 2 minutes, I'm being given the disappointment of her silence. There was no sense in both of us pretending that this wasn't happening, so finally I said, "Your phone is ringing, you want me to get that?" Of course the answer was "no". I couldn't quite figure out why though.

That was a joke, by the way. I have too much respect for personal space to answer someone else's phone. But I did demand an explanation. I shouldn't have had to, but I did. Of course, he was just a friend. The usual questions followed. What kind of friend, especially a man, not only calls at this time of night, but calls repeatedly, if he truly is just a friend that's not looking for anything else? Is this "friendship" sexual in nature? Because if he's down for whatever sexually, I have news: he's not a friend. And because I'm smarter than the average bear, and even the above average bear, she couldn't use the emergency excuse. If it were an emergency, she wouldn't have reacted so calmly when she realized it was him. She wouldn't have allowed him to blow up her phone without checking to see if everything was okay. This told me that not only was this "friend" okay, but this type of behavior was par for the course.

I'm sure that many of you can identify with what happened to me. You're sitting there trying to explain to someone that claims to love you that you deserve respect and they shouldn't have other men or women calling them all times of the night. Meanwhile, that cell phone is still blowing up in the background while they're trying to convince you that they don't know why this is happening. Well, if you're just as surprised as I am, then why not answer the phone and address it right now? If that's not an option, then you should do what you can to be sure that this never happens again. But most importantly, one way or another, we should have a discussion about this as opposed to me hoping that you understand my displeasure at what's going on and that you'll just find it in your heart to do the right thing. If you had that in your heart, we wouldn't be here listening to this phone buzzing away like an overpopulated beehive.

Sometimes our partners have the good sense to know that they've screwed up and they need to apologize and make things right. But when dealing with people that tend to lie or cheat, they need direction to the land of Do The Right Thing. The problem that I had is that this wasn't the first time this had happened and if I didn't do something for myself instead of waiting for this individual to do the right thing, it would happen again. Sometimes you can trust people and sometimes you can trust them to be who they are. Sometimes, we as humans aren't at our best. If your eyes are open to that, I can't promise that you'll never be hurt, but at least you'll be better prepared.

Now, after saying all of that, I'm very well aware that sometimes we give those digits to the wrong people. Sometimes, a person just takes it upon themselves to be obsessive. Sometimes, it's beyond your control. Understanding all of that, we must understand that we still have a responsibility to our relationship and to the people we're involved with. In certain situations in life, apologies are in order even if it's not your fault. Something I wrote about in my first book is the absence of honesty in relationships. Honesty isn't just something that needs to be preserved in the exclusive relationship. It needs to be preserved in all relationships. It's important when starting a new relationship or just dating. But the honesty hasn't just gone from relationships between a man and a woman. It's disappeared from all of our relationships as a whole. Friendships have suffered at the hands of dishonesty as well.

As for the male/female end of the equation, we tend to think that the only people we need to be honest with are people that we're exclusive with. However, it's important to be honest with people that we just dating or "kickin' it" with. We've become so afraid of being open with people that we haven't committed to that we'd rather just lie. All along forgetting that one lie leads to another, and if you start out a relationship on a lie, even one that doesn't have a commitment, you have to continue the lie. And sooner or later, it will be found out. I know that in a new relationship or when we're dating, we like to protect ourselves and not give too much of ourselves away too fast, but you can have honesty without full disclosure. We must rediscover the honor in being honest with one another.

With each lie that we tell one another, whether it is in an exclusive relationship, one we hope to be exclusive someday or a friendship, we bring uncertainty and a sense of insecurity the situation. But what the dishonest soon find out is that insecurity is a two-way street. If you continue to receive those late night phone calls, it won't be long before your partner begins to receive some phone calls of their own. And that's when the real fun begins because there's no one more insecure than the cheater because they know that Karma and retribution is coming. One doesn't have to be seeking revenge against you in order for you to feel its sting. Just something to think about.

Now for those of you that have friends that can't seem to solve their own problems and will constantly call you at all hours of the night to discuss their problems, there comes a point where you have to let people know that you aren't a counselor (unless, of course, you are, then you should let them know what your office hours are). It's okay to be there for a friend, but if it starts to affect your relationship, you need to have a talk and a true friend will understand.

Friends: How many of us have them?

Speaking of friends, what happened to them? And I'm not talking about Ross, Joey and Chandler from the sitcom *Friends* here. I'm talking about our friends. The status of the friend has changed dramatically over the years. People aren't there for one another like they used to be. They still claim to be, but it's not quite the same. And what's worse, we're stabbing each other in the back at an alarming rate. So that causes me to ask (or rap) that old question that Whodini asked on that hip hop classic many, many years ago: Friends, how many of us have them?

As usual, with most things I write, this came about from a personal experience. Not too long ago, I had a disagreement with someone that I thought was a friend about what the true level and definition of friendship should be and what one's responsibility are to said friendship. It didn't end well as we both seemed to be ending our friendship. I've known this person for over 20 years, so we're not talking about some fly-by-night friendship here. But at the same time, if the commitment to be a friend isn't there, then what is it?

In my world, the definition of a friend reads like this: A friend is someone that you can call on day or night and if they can't help you with whatever you're going through, they will be there to try and see you through. If they can't be contacted right away, like being on hold with the cable company or any other service, "your call is important to them". If they can't pick up, they always call back. Because you're never too busy for a true friend. You may not be able to answer when they call all the time, but you always hit 'em back.

While there are some circumstances and friendships that are exceptions to the rule, most true friends won't go months without speaking to you. True friends are concerned about your well-being, so not checking on you for two or three months doesn't make sense. You could've lost a loved one, a job or your sense of purpose in life. These are all things that a true friend should be around to help you get through. They can be a shoulder to lean on or just lend an ear. You can't do those things when you only talk once per quarter of the year.

A friend is someone that you can tell things to in confidence and not worry about all of your business winding up in the streets. Now, let's be real. We all tell things that we shouldn't tell, but you don't tell the big ones. For example, she may tell another one of her girls that you and him finally did it last night, but she won't tell 'em that you're late in a month.

Many people have many views and points of view on this subject. For example, one of the things she and I disagreed on is how often friends should be in contact. She said to me that friends should be able to go months without contacting one another, and when they come back together, it should be all good. I may be in the minority, but I disagree. I'll explain.

When I was younger, I was taught that you have basically 3 separate groups: friends, associates/acquaintances and people you don't deal with. I think what's happened over the years is we've blurred the line just like we have with the words "need" and "want". We've mixed all of these people up and now we can't tell one from another. We're calling associates friends, treating friends like people we don't care about and unnecessarily elevating some to the level of friendship when they aren't deserving. At the same time, we're allowing people to call themselves friends without correction, when they haven't fulfilled the role of friend.

There used to be a time when you called on a friend and they'd be right there. And if they weren't, you knew you couldn't call them a friend and they understood that. With the case of me and my "friend", I had a similar situation. I asked her to be there for my family during a difficult time and she assured me that she would do anything that I needed her to do. However, when I asked her had she done what she said she would, she told me she hadn't because she was too busy. In my mind, this put a new face on our friendship. I didn't feel that I could count on her in my time of need, even if she gave her word, and it changed the way I saw her. Based on our recent conversation, I don't think she really cares how I see her anymore.

On the other side of this thing, how many times have you heard of or saw on TV a best friend sleeping with a friend's husband, wife or lover? I'm not saying that these things have just started recently. Friends have been screwing over friends for years. But they never used to try and convince you that it was still all good after the fact. All involved knew the friendship was over. Only an associate would think otherwise.

In reality, you'll only have one or two real friends in your entire lifetime. The rest are just a part of the landscape of life. Though necessary in some cases, not necessarily worthy of the title of "friend". We all like to elevate our status sometimes so that we feel more important. Being a friend carries a lot more weight than these other titles, just like manager does in relation to assistant manager. But just like titles on the job, you must either earn them or do special favors to get them. We've all been selfish and prideful enough to make ourselves someone's friend when we would never fulfill that role if put to the test. Some people are just associates and we all need to understand that it's okay to be one.

If you're not willing to fill the role of true friend, don't assume the title. In relation to me and my "friend", I don't see it as a lost friendship because I can see now that it had already been lost long ago. We were just making the assumption that because we had known each other for years that the title would and should always apply. But longevity doesn't mean entitlement. Not on my part and not on hers. From my perspective, you can still have love for someone that you've known for a long time. But we all must understand that over time, relationships change based on what's being given and what's needed. Some might suggest that there are different levels of friendship and that's a point I'm willing to consider. But like it or not, friendships, whether real or semi-real, have obligations. And if you can't fulfill them, then maybe it's time for reassignment to the associates department of the company. Or maybe I'm just overreacting.

Chapter 4

Still Disconnected: Are you ready for a (spiritual) revolution?

In the beginning, my primary motivation for writing this book was to explore the two sides of my personality. I wanted to try and give the world a glimpse into a lighter side of myself after showing a more serious side of myself in my first book. As I was going through and looking at all of the things that make up who I am, I came to a few conclusions. First, there are waaaaay more than two sides to me. It's like some weird kind of Rubik's Cube inside there. But what I also discovered is there are probably two or more sides to all of us. I'm not alone in this walk of duality.

When faced with the things that life can bring you, we're usually going to react one of two ways. That's why I say that there are at least two sides to all of us. Whatever we may be going through at the time will usually determine how we will react. For lack of better terms, depending on what's happening, we may take the high road and we may take the low road. There's a right way and a wrong way. There's a righteous way and a sinner's way.

There's God's way and there's the way of the world. Believe it or not, both are necessary. We'd all like things to be peaceful at all times, but sometimes life will take you to that other side. And sometimes, that's the way it needs to be. You have to get a little "worldly" with some people sometimes just to let 'em know that they can't just mistreat you and move on with their day. Now, you don't have to curse them out, but you do have to let 'em know. Just replace a few words here and there and you'll make your point.

The problem of the good angel on one shoulder and a devil on the other isn't a new one. All of the choices in life aren't defined that way, but there are critical decisions that we make in our lives that are. Some of the things that hang in the balance are whether or not to cheat, whether or not to steal and whether or not we should treat our fellow man right. Which side we choose to listen to is often determined by the situations we're in or by the circumstances we're facing. We all know the difference between right and wrong. However, knowing is only half the battle. Just because we know right from wrong doesn't mean that we'll always make sound judgment.

Over the years, we have begun to favor the wrong over the right more and more. We've become too willing to take an eye for an eye, never accepting the fact that we will all be blind soon. We as a people have lost our connection with God. It's something that I touched on in my first book, but really didn't delve into because the nature and focus of that book was healing the black family and relationships through the correction of our own behavior. But without the guidance of the Almighty, we have no chance at loosening the grip of those things that bind us.

We've become so caught up in arguing over who is God, who's really saved and who's not and/or what we should and shouldn't be teaching in the church, that we've completely lost all sense of our spiritual side and its need to be nurtured. I feel that some of these discussions are necessary to have (as you'll see in the coming pages), but our central themes need to remain in tact and I think we've lost that. We're so strong in the fight that we have begun to neglect our spiritual side. Our spiritual side is the side that keeps us from doing wrong when we should be doing right. It's the side of us that reminds us of the shame in certain behaviors. It's the side of us that keeps us in check. It's your direct connection with God.

What I want to cover in this chapter and over the next few are some of the ways that we've not only lost our connection with God, but how we've lost our connection with one another. For example, one of the main problems that we have, especially in the black community, is that we don't go to church anymore. We don't go as individuals and we don't go as a family. Now, if you're reading this and you're not of the Christian faith, that's okay. Whatever faith you follow, we're all faced with the same dilemma. People don't go to any particular place of worship anymore. At a time when we need a Higher Power the most, we've decided to turn away and go it alone. Going to our place of worship is something that we need for spiritual purposes and for the purpose of just coming together and fellowshipping with one another. We've allowed to world and all of its misery to invade us, take over our thoughts and disconnect us from our God.

One of the reasons that people have gone away from the church is because of the hypocrisy that appears to be there. People in the church aren't living the way they say they're living and the world knows it. People in the church are claiming to be things that they aren't. Now, this isn't something new, but it has become more prevalent. The culture of greed and money worship has also crept into the walls of the synagogue. Again, that perception of the church isn't new, but it has become more prevalent. Our churches have gotten bigger and there's nothing wrong with big churches as long as it's to God's glory. But is that really the case?

As our churches have gotten bigger, so have our houses. Our cars have gotten more expensive. On the surface, it appears that a street culture has made its way into the pulpit. We can't tell rappers, pimps and preachers apart. To be honest, there were always similarities between the preacher and the pimp. They both seemed to be wearing the finest garments and driving the nicest cars. The difference used to be what happened when they opened their mouths. The difference used to be what they were teaching you. One talked about salvation and the other talked about sensations.

There's nothing wrong with people of faith living the good life, but what are we teaching our people when they come to church? Are we arming them with the Word of God so that they can make it in this cruel world that we live in? In an effort to keep up with the Joneses or the hip hoppers, have we sold God out for a message of bling? How has this disconnection with the soul affected our world, our culture, our individual lives and how we treat one another? And finally, have we allowed the street culture to lead us astray, as opposed to us leading the streets to a path of living right? Let's talk.

Seeking a new balance

Just as this book is split into two halves and it started with the poem "Gemini" from my poetry book *Scenes From The Blue Book*, most of us are operating under two sides. I'm sure that most of you haven't gone as far as I have and given them names, but I'm sure it's there. What you can usually do is divide them down lines of spirituality and the secular.

What brought about my first book and eventually this one is a level of spiritual maturity that I found myself in need of. The older we get, the more mature we're supposed to become. That maturity is supposed to keep coming until we leave here. We're supposed to go from growing up to growing old gracefully. As I took a look at my people in my earlier work, it caused me to look at myself. That was the purpose of the work. For all of us, myself included, to take a look at what we were, what we've become and what we need to be. We all needed to re-examine and take an honest look at ourselves. That work was quite therapeutic for me and now I'm on a quest to take further steps to reach a balance in my life that, up until recently, has gone missing. There needs to be a different kind of marriage ceremony in my life. One different from the one that my sisters and my mother continue to push for. There needs to be a marriage of the mind, body and spirit. Not only for me, but for all of us.

As we go through our adult years, one side of our personality is supposed become more prominent than the other. What that requires is letting go of or gaining more control of one side of ourselves. This is easier said than done. The reason that we sometimes can't stop doing wrong is because what's wrong usually feels so good. Again, it doesn't matter if you're a person of faith or not. It also doesn't matter what you consider wrong based on your values system. It seems to feel better than doing what you feel is right.

For example, I often find myself in conflict because I still love some hip hop music. Not to the degree that I used to because I feel that the true spirit of the music has been killed by materialism and misogyny, but it's still prominent in my iPod. I may not run out and buy as much as I used to, but some of the stuff that I listened to back in the day still gets played. I escaped the effects that it's had on some of our young men and how they treat and speak to our women, but does it make it okay for me to continue to listen just because I'm wise enough not to infuse it into my everyday life? I really don't know. One has to wonder if the sin is listening to something that would be offensive and degrading to others or brining it out into the world by living the lyrics.

Hip hop used to be something that simply came with being young and black. But the reality is that some of the elements that exist in the music are threatening to who we are as a people. I don't want this to turn into a dissertation on hip hop because I covered some of that in my first two books and maybe I'll cover it in it's entirety in a future book. But there are some days when I listen to the lyrics and I feel like I'm betraying black women. I sometimes feel that I should stop listening just for the sake of my beautiful black women out there. I've even gotten to the point where if I'm on a date, I don't even consider rap music as a choice while we're riding along. But what makes it hard is the fact that our women have gravitated toward the music just as men do. Songs that *should* be offensive to them are being embraced by them. There are songs that women listen to nowadays that I'm actually offended by. Is this a sign of maturity or am I losing my East Side of Detroit edge?

As I try to connect with the spiritual side of who I am, I can't help but ask these questions. As I attempt to change course in my life once again, I wonder how much of the old me I will have to let go of. Surely when we change we have to let go of some of the old to embrace the new, but the question is always how much. Sometimes we have to lose part of ourselves in order to discover something new, but we don't wanna give up everything. It's like paying bills when you're struggling. The wise thing to do is to pay the bill off completely so that you won't have to worry about it hanging over your head. But sometimes, we'll pay that minimum amount due just to keep a few dollars in our pocket.

We also concern ourselves with the opinion of others when considering a change in our lives. Too many times we're afraid to walk a straight and narrow path because of what others may think of us. Even at older ages, we're victims of peer pressure. You may be a causal drinker that tends to get drunk when in the company of other drinkers. You may be one that chooses their words carefully when pushed to anger, but you swear like a sailor when you're around your boys in an effort to assert your manhood. Or maybe you're one that treats your woman like the queen that she is until you're around some that may view that behavior as soft, and then you suddenly change.

If you were raised like I was, you have a spiritual foundation. You have a sense of what God expects of you. That doesn't mean that you'll always be living right. That doesn't mean that you won't stray. That doesn't mean that you won't make mistakes or fall victim to some of the things I mentioned in the last paragraph. What it does mean is that when you fall victim to all of the pitfalls of simply being human, you probably know better. Making a mistake isn't the end of the world. The problem is knowing that you've made that mistake and doing nothing to correct it. What's worse is straying from your foundation because of what others may think of you.

When we think of making the changes that I'm talking about here, we're usually talking about the spiritual vs. the secular. One of the reasons that we're resistant to putting down things of a secular nature is because there's a perception that picking up things of a spiritual nature is boring. We believe that people that are spiritual in nature have no fun. All they do is go to church and all they talk about is God. Though that is the case with some who walk away from the secular world, it's not true with everyone. Spirituality isn't always a church thing or a religious thing. Spirituality is about a connection that one has with their soul. It's about the connection that your soul has with a Higher Power. There are people in the world that are very spiritual, but not necessarily entrenched in the church.

We also make the assumption that everything that's secular in nature is bad for you. The women and men seem hotter in the secular world, the music is allegedly better, R-rated movies seem so much more fun because you can relate. That will always be the struggle. Believing that you can have a good, fulfilling and even fun life without all the stress of living in the secular world. But we must come to understand that we can enjoy some things that exist in the world without putting our souls in danger. For example, there's nothing wrong with a good love song, but maybe the lust songs that have become so prominent can conflict with a spirit that's attempting to move away from some things that are worldly.

What I'm coming to terms with is the two halves that make up the whole of me. As I said, being spiritual isn't always a religious experience. It's about connecting with yourself on a higher level. It's about being above what you see on a day to day basis. It's about not being defined by what this world has to offer you in this life, and trying to connect with what we have waiting for us in the next. Knowing that we have another life waiting for us *should* change the behavior we exhibit in this life. That's not always what I see when I look at myself and others.

Letting go of all of the negative things that the world has to offer isn't something that you just wake up and do. It's a process. To me, it isn't something that you do to put others down or to say "Shame on you" to those in the world. It's a personal journey that you must go on. When we go on this journey, we often think that we have to head straight to the church and read the Bible for the rest of our days. But I don't think that's the journey I'm on. The journey I'm on includes a better relationship with God, but it doesn't end there. I can still enjoy some of the fruits of life without being degrading to women, using language that's less than flattering or being involved in things that can harm me physically.

I think that's one of the things that kept me from marrying all these years. Along with the lack of quality choices, my refusal to settle for less because the choices aren't of the same quality as they used to be and my sometimes quiet and withdrawn personality, in recent years, I've been too busy trying to marry those elements that I spoke of before. I'm too busy trying to marry my mind, body and spirit so that they might walk in harmony. I can't know if my woman's mind ain't right if my mind ain't right. I can't discern whether or not she's got a body fit for a King if I haven't respected the kingdom that is my body. And I can't lead my family spiritually if my spirit isn't aligned with the heavens above.

And though my spirit must be aligned with the heavens above, I still exist in the flesh and I must find a way to maintain in this world so that I'll be right for the next. All of the elements that make up me must be acknowledged, embraced when necessary and discarded when not necessary. They all serve a purpose. Some serve as a reminder of what I want to and should be. Some serve as a reminder of where I've come from and what I no longer need to be.

We must eliminate the fear that we have of leading a more grounded and spiritual life. We're so afraid of criticism that we sometimes continue to walk the same roads, even though we can see that those roads lead to nowhere. You have the make the right choices for your future life *and* the afterlife. We can't operate based on what others think of us or to appease others. If you lose some friends along the way, and I can assure you that you will, it's okay. If you get some funny looks from some people, that's okay too. When you refuse to bow to the ways of the world, you will stand out because there aren't very many out there like you. I can attest to the fact that you will spend some time alone, as I have lost some people on my quest to enlightenment. But I'm a firm believer that God will replace all those that have left me with something of a little more substance.

"You think you're better than me?"

One of the most seemingly offensive things we can say or suggest to someone is that we're better than they are. It suggests a certain arrogance to think such things. If you were to openly admit that you felt that way, you could see the mouths dropping open, hear the gasps and see the eyebrows raise faster than The Rock's back when he was the wrestler The Rock telling you to "know your role and shut your mouth", and not the movie star The Rock who plays a football coach (predictable), a bounty hunter (also predictable) and an aspiring Hollywood actor/bodyguard who's secretly gay (huh?). Yes, if you told someone that you were better than they were, you'd hear this response from the 'burbs to the 'hood: "You think you're better than me?"

Those that know me personally know that one of my favorite phrases is "Sometimes, the answer is no". Conversely, sometimes the answer is yes. If you wanna know if some of us are better than others, the answer is a resounding yes. You're better financially, better physically, better emotionally and better spiritually. This is critical information and it should be used to the good. The problem is it's not always used that way.

Knowing that you're better than someone isn't a reason to rub their faces in it. It's not an excuse to look down on someone. It's not enabling you with a God-given right to let it be known every second of the day. God has given some of us more than others for a reason, but I doubt that reason was to put down others. We were put here to be much more than that. We weren't put here to be the bane of another's existence. To quote my first book, these powers must be used for good, and never evil.

God put us at different stages of life to show others the way to go. We all have something to offer those that are coming up behind us. Coming up in the sense of those that are younger and those that are walking the path that we have walked. Yes, we do have the ability to be better than others, but we should all take on the responsibility of showing others how to arrive to a destination that we have already reached. Not by looking down your nose at them. Not by putting them down. Not by flaunting ourselves.

By simply imparting wisdom gained, sharing life experiences and showing the blueprint to our successes. As for those with the aspirations of reaching those statuses, you mustn't harden your heart to knowledge. You must be willing to learn.

Once again, something that comes to mind is the current state of my beloved hip hop music. What has become commonplace is the so-called beef that these rappers all seem to have with one another. This guy doesn't like that guy, this crew doesn't like that crew. Arguments have started over things as silly as tattoos, who's from what side of town and the ever present female persuasion. It's amazing how they can refer to women as "bitches" and "hos" all over their records, but as soon as one of these women leaves one for the other, they wanna fight about it. But, I digress.

For all of the business savvy that these guys claim to and sometimes seem to have, they haven't quite figured out how to divide the entertainment pie. It's never made any sense to me that one rapper would hate another rapper so much that he had to go out and make a record putting that guy down. Now, on the surface, it all seems to be male machismo and all about street cred, but what they really want to do is end the other guy's career. Sometimes just to be cruel, but sometimes because the other guy is real competition, which in my opinion, is something that most of these rappers can't handle. But rather than do what most businesses do and build a better mouse trap, or in this case, be a better rapper, they hurl insults at their enemies hoping that we'll stop buying his records and he'll fade into obscurity. In the past, that's what happened in hip hop, but not just because of one rapper's dominance over the other. In my opinion, if a rapper faded into obscurity, he simply wasn't good enough. But things are different these days.

With the industry at an all time high financially, these things make no sense to me. In the past, there were very few rappers that made a lot of hit records, and thus, a lot of money. So the competition for those very few lucrative recording contracts that major labels were willing to give to this "fad" was fierce. You had to be head and shoulders above the rest, and maybe even seek to eliminate your competition. Nowadays, not only are there more than enough rap contracts to go around (in fact, there are a few too many and some need to be eliminated), the rappers are actually in charge in some cases. Those that were smart enough found themselves in positions of power so that they might help others over the fence. Though competition is always fierce and just a part of life, do we still need to be so cutthroat and isn't there enough room for all of us now?

The deaths of Biggie and 2pac seem to have taught them nothing. It makes no sense to make consumers choose in this current hip hop climate. Why make a 15 year old boy divide his loyalty between two rappers and sometimes his own friends (yes, this kind of infighting does affect a consumer's friendship with another if he's overly loyal to a particular rapper and his friend is overly loyal to the other side)? When I was 15, I didn't have the wisdom to know that I didn't have to choose one rapper over the other, and I doubt today's 15 year olds have that same wisdom. Just as they do in high school with their little cliques, they divide their loyalties, which is what these rappers want. But what the rapper is missing out on is a fan, more exposure and more of the money that they so covet. What the fan is missing is the music.

Even as an adult, because I was more of a Biggie fan, I found myself put off by 2pac because of his dislike of Biggie and it took me a while to finally let it go and embrace both sides. Imagine what a younger mind does. Because we have become so greedy as a people and as a society, we dare not allow our fans to purchase *both* albums. We demand that they choose sides. You can't be down with me if you're down with him. This crap only exists in hip hop. I couldn't imagine, say, The Isley Brothers and The O'Jays going through such foolishness. If every rapper had abandoned this attitude, they all probably would have sold 500, 000 to 1 million more albums because the fans wouldn't be choosing sides, and they might actually buy both your albums. But because we don't have the ability to help each other along, or at the very least follow mama's advice when she said "If you can't say nothin' nice…", we cut off our nose to spite our face.

What does this all have to do with what we're supposed to be talking about, you ask? If I'm better than you with money, life, spirituality, rapping or whatever, is it so wrong for me to offer you some advice along the way? If you're willing to listen, isn't the world of success big enough for you and I? And if you're not willing to listen, can't I just walk away and leave it be without calling you every kind of stupid in the book?

We as blacks used to share a sense of togetherness. We used to be so willing to help each other along in life. It's obvious to me that those days are long behind us. In the past, we were all we had so we had to stick together. In the south, in those cotton fields, we had to be about each other. But something changed when we came north. We adapted to the kill or be killed way of the streets. To quote a line from a poem I wrote called "A Prayer To Black Jesus", "There's only so much of his freedom that a man can exercise if he's really to remain free". Once we became allegedly free, we begin to separate.

This goes back to the lack of connection that I spoke about moments ago. We'd rather fight and try to kill one another than help each another. I understand that some of what I've said goes against some of the rules of business, but this isn't a matter of this or that. What I'm saying is there is enough for all of us. If a person chooses not to buy my book, it shouldn't be because a "rival" black author spent half of his book putting my work down. If he doesn't like what I've said, then he shouldn't buy it. But should he go out and discourage others from buying it? I don't think so. Maybe I wasn't able to reach him, but it may have a different effect on another person. Years ago, I had a website and there was a section on it dedicated to music. I only posted reviews of music that I enjoyed. I wanted to promote, not destroy. If I didn't like your album or your music, I didn't waste a single word talking about it.

I understand that some things are a matter of business and competition and there's nothing you can do about it. But there are some things that we as blacks need to stop fighting about. All of the jealousies, the hatred and the desire to see each other fail need to be done away with. I understand that all of us joining hands and marching together is just a pipe dream, but we should at least be able to cease our attempts to destroy each other, all to the satisfaction of a section of society that feels that we're self destructive anyway. I spoke earlier about the eye for an eye mentality that we have. Sometimes, people will say or do things that we don't like. We need to develop that side of us that turns the other cheek. We need to develop a sense of unity. And if we can't do that, we need to develop the courage to walk away without intentionally damaging one another.

"Let the church say prosperity..."

Over the years we have experienced a growth in the "mega

church" in this country, especially in the black community. There was a time in my youth when there were but a few of these churches and they were usually run by old white men. You'd see them on TV and hear them on the radio. "The power of Christ compels you!" they'd say, usually with a southern twang in their voices. They'd preach and then ask you to be a prayer partner by sending in a small "gift of faith", "seed of faith" or "whatever of faith" in hopes that your life would turn around.

There was something about the whole thing that seemed to be wrong. A guy on TV that just talked for about 30 to 45 minutes and now I have to send him money to improve my life? Why? Isn't my life better if I keep the money? I see you there on the screen, your lovely wife by your side, all dressed in your beautiful garments and you don't *seem* to be in need of my money. And just when all of your doubts seem to be at their peak, "the power of Christ compels you" and you're reaching for the check book, an envelope and your book of stamps (that tells you how far back I'm going; who mails letters anymore?)

Of course, this is nothing new. The man of God has always been under suspicion. How many people believed everything Moses said? He couldn't even get down off that mountain before those once enslaved Israelites had built a golden calf and started praying to it (something that we as blacks continue to do today and yet we wonder why God isn't pleased with our behavior). How many people believed what Noah had to say when he was building that ark? How 'bout Job when he wouldn't give up on God the way we do when God doesn't do exactly what we say, when we say? Or what about Jesus Christ? They crucified Him for being who He was. Even if I were to indulge those who don't believe that He was the Messiah, He simply claimed to be the Son of God and if we're all God's children, wasn't He still technically correct? I'm one of God's sons and I hope the mob isn't on its way to see me.

The preacher has always faced skepticism. Every time the offering plate is passed, eyes are rolled in the church. Every time the pastor has a new suit on or gets a new car, someone starts talking. We see the preacher at the grocery store and we instantly believe that our particular $15 donation is what's paying for those pork chops in his basket. "Where'd he get the money for that food?" we ask under our breath. And this wasn't something that just happened to the pastors of large churches. This is something that happened everywhere.

Fast forward to today and now we have high profile preachers all over the country, all over radio, all over the internet and all over TV. Churches with thousands and thousands of members are commonplace. So if you think the skeptics were out for Rev. So-and-so who simply had a hundred members and a small community church in the 'hood, you can imagine what's happening now when Rev. Big Time has 10,000 members, God knows how many watching on TV and he's driving a Bentley through the suburbs. Is all of the skepticism fair and are we right to pass judgment?

Judging from a distance

"... Touch not mine anointed and do my prophets no harm"
— Psalm 105:15

This isn't the part of the book where I take all of the preachers to task. My pastor is Rev. Dan Flowers of the Zion Hill Baptist Church of Detroit, MI. He's also my uncle. He's always taught me to be careful how you deal with God's preacher. Because of those teachings, I don't feel that it's my place to correct a man that says he's been called into the ministry by God. Whether he's telling the truth or not is between that man and God. I'm not here to call out those that I think are using their position in the church to abuse people, have unholy relationships with them or steal from them. There are certain radio hosts, ministers, authors and such, who will also remain nameless, that feel that they should call them out and that it's okay. But I believe firmly in the Bible when it says judge not, lest ye be judged. We have to be careful when we remove the cover off of another lest we be exposed as well. There are parts of all of us that we'd rather the world didn't know about. You may not have stolen millions from a congregation, but is your infidelity any less shameful? Maybe it is in the eyes of man, but not in the eyes of the Almighty.

This is also not being written to tear down the mega churches that exist. I do have my suspicions about some of these preaches in some of those churches, but I'm also a believer in some others that run some of those churches. The reality of the situation is that some of them are living right and some of them aren't. I'm not willing to believe that they're all right or all wrong. Just like those of us outside of the ministry, there are some that are living right and some that aren't. We like to assume and pretend that just because someone has been called into the ministry that they're not subject to the same pitfalls that we suffer in our lives. Let's not be fooled, they too are still human.

We also make the assumption that a crooked preacher only exists in the mega churches, and that's simply not true. In fact, there are some in the mega churches that are more righteous than some in the smaller churches. I've seen some unsavory things with my own two eyes in a so-called mega church *and* some smaller churches that exist in my own city. The reason that some of these perceptions exist is because we as humans have a knack for passing judgment on things that we have no knowledge of. Before we've walked a mile in someone's shoes, or better yet, sat in someone's church service to see what's really going on there, we immediately assume that we know what's going on from a distance. Based on that preacher's car, his manner of dress and where he's living, he must be doing something dirty.

It's natural to have some suspicions when you see something that doesn't look right or doesn't feel right. If you feel uncomfortable, I think it's not only okay, but necessary that you don't worship in a particular church. We should all be made to feel comfortable when serving our God and if what's going on in a particular church doesn't mesh well with your spirit, then it's imperative that you move on to another place. There is more than one church or pastor here on earth that can help you get to heaven. You have to go where God leads you and I don't believe it's His desire for us to worship in discomfort. But we must remember not to decide based on perception or what you may have heard (I'll get to that in a minute). Just as we should study and know the Word for ourselves, we should do some research and visit a church before believing what everybody else says about it.

Spread the Word and the wealth

Over time, folks began to wonder how a man who claims to be following the Word of God (which suggests in Mark 10:21 that we should sell our belongings and give to the poor and we shall have treasures in Heaven, and then take up our cross and follow Him), could be living so lavish. If a preacher is supposed to be helping the poor, then why is he so "rich"? If we're all supposed to give 'til it hurts in church, why doesn't he seem to be hurting just as I am? And above all, how can I be down?

From my perspective, once some of these preachers started to hear those questions and feel the heat from their particular congregations, they began to go infomercial on us. They started telling us "You too can live like this!" This is as old as time itself. If people begin to question you about how you got rich, especially if you're seemingly getting rich off of them and some of them are poor and disenfranchised, there's one sure fire way to get them off your back or keep them from robbing you to exact some measure of revenge: Tell them how they can get rich too.

What preachers began to do is tell these people that they can have all of the desires of their heart, which is what it says in the Bible, if they simply ask God for it. But this isn't some new and exciting message that they were preaching. This message has always been in effect. As I said, this is Bible. If we ask God to grant us the desires of our heart, He will do it. These preachers aren't outside of the Word of God when they say these things. God wants to bless us with the finer things in life. But dealing with God is no different than dealing with your job on a day-to-day basis. If you wanna go further, you gotta do some work. God has requirements for us to meet in order to receive His blessings.

From my point of view, what happened over time is preachers began to leave out certain elements that existed in the Bible as it pertains to God blessing us. To put it in general terms, the main requirement that God has for blessing us is that we live right. God is not in the business of blessing just for the sake of blessing. Because He is a graceful and merciful God, He will bless us when we aren't deserving. But in order to continue to receive those blessings, we have to be worthy of those blessings.

Does that mean that some will *appear* to be blessed when they probably aren't deserving? Of course. Just as I said about our jobs, we all know someone that was promoted when they either didn't deserve it or weren't ready. I don't know about you, but it happens weekly on my job. But what appears to be a blessing isn't always so. A drug dealer has nice clothes and nice cars, but is he really blessed when he can't go near his family for fear that someone might kill them simply for being related to him? Is he blessed when at any point of any day of his life his deeds may find him in the way of gunfire that's meant to end his life? If that's a blessed life, then I don't need that blessing.

As the churches and the messages continued to change, certain elements began to become a regular part of a preacher's sermon, while other very important elements began to disappear. The term "prosperity preachers" began to become more common. If you thought the pin-stripped suits and Cadillacs of the past were flashy, then you'd better make way. All of that was replaced by bright colored suits, gator shoes, Lexus', Mercedes' and Bentleys, million dollar homes and in some cases, private planes. Yes, God is good. Real good.

As churches grew, we began to hear more and more about the financial goodness of God. It wasn't just about Sunday School anymore, it was about business school. The church had always been a business and you have to run it as such or it will fail. But who knew that we'd ever hear our pastor talking about diversified funds and portfolios from the pulpit? Aren't chains and diamonds like that reserved for the rappers, ballplayers and pimps of the world and not the man of God? That is a nice car reverend and I don't mean to be all in your business, but who *is* paying for it?

These are all of the questions that are whispered in the church, and screamed outside of it. And though it may be unfair at some points, it's understandable at others. In an effort to show their people how they could attain some of the finer things in life, preachers started to preach more and more about money and how we need to go about getting it. There seemed to be a sense that God wanted all of us to live like the pastor was living. Every sermon seemed to be more and more about what God has for us here on earth and less and less about what God has for us when we get home.

There seemed to be more about living for right now as opposed to living for the afterlife. The old school preachers always talked about living right so that we can see the Kingdom of God. The new school preachers seemed to be talking about living right now and getting all that we can here on earth. From this, we all began to split. Though we were always split down denominational lines, we all used to have two things in common: Our overall message about God and the desire to see His Kingdom. We have division now because our message is divided.

"And Jesus knew their thoughts, and said unto them, 'Every kingdom divided against itself is brought to desolation; and every city or house divided against itself shall not stand'" –
Matthew 12:25

In my opinion, there's nothing wrong with preaching about prosperity. God wants us to be prosperous. High living isn't something that He simply saved for the secular. We can live in fine houses and drive fine cars as well. We don't have to live a meager lifestyle in order to be in the will of God. I'm no better because I wouldn't spend a quarter of a million dollars on any car even if I had it. That's just my preference. But I believe that God wants me to be able to if I choose to. There's nothing wrong with preachers showing their congregation that it's okay to strive for the best in life, especially in the black community where we only see it in the drug dealers, pimps, athletes and rappers. If a minister is truly a man of God, he can be a positive role model in this sense. The real question is what is he really teaching you and is it *all* that God wants him to teach you?

While we have become completely focused on the earthly possessions, we've forgotten one very important element: Jesus. Now granted, I haven't attended all of the mega churches that exist in the world, but that's okay. Because they're all over the TV and the internet, I don't have to. I can sit in my living room and see what they're all talking about. The thing I noticed the most is that Jesus seems to have disappeared from their sermons. There isn't as much talk about going to Heaven as there is about seeking some measure of heaven here on earth. The only time they seem to be focused on Christ is during the Christmas message and the Easter message. Being saved doesn't seem as important as being rich anymore. What happened to messages of making sure your soul is saved because you can't take your material possessions with you? They seemed to have gone the way of the pin-stripped suit.

These are just my thoughts and I don't intend to judge or bring anybody down, but as far as I'm concerned, any message that's missing Jesus is incomplete. We as Christians do need to understand that it's okay to have wealth, but if all we're doing is teaching them about gettin' paid and not teaching them about gettin' saved, the goodness of God, the blood of Jesus and how we are saved by it and how we should live right as opposed to just living rich, we're delivering an incomplete message to the people. What good would it do me to teach my son that he can have a prosperous life but never show him an example of the hard work that it will take to achieve that? As I've told my son, a dream without action is just an incomplete thought. If I don't teach him a complete lesson, he will seek a short cut to success. There are no elevators to the top. We all have to take the stairs. Teaching our people about the money and the material possessions without teaching them about real salvation is doing them a disservice. There are no short cuts to heaven and you certainly can't buy or drive your way in.

All of these perceptions about the church come from somewhere, and it's usually from within the church. If there's a rumor about a pastor that's misusing his position in the church, having a sexual affair or allegedly stealing from the church, it was probably started by a member or a former member that either saw something that they couldn't understand or had something done to them in that church that they didn't like and now they're seeking revenge. So while we question the pastor, we need to learn to question ourselves or question the information we're receiving. If you don't go to church to be spiritually fed and serve your God, then why do you go?

This goes back to what I said I was taught by my pastor and the verse that I quoted from Psalms. You have to be careful how you speak about the man of God. Now, where some of us screw up is in making our own determinations on who actually is the man of God. Something else my pastor taught me is that we don't know who God has ordained to speak for Him. So the fact that we don't always feel that a particular preacher is a man of God shouldn't make us say what we say about them. I'm not going to pretend that I don't struggle with this issue sometimes, but God is still working with me just as He is with you.

While we're at church, our focus should be on God and the message. Now, I didn't say messenger. I said the message. We get caught up in the messenger too often and we wind up missing what God has for us. As I stated earlier, we forget that even though a minister has been called by God to preach His Word, he's still just an imperfect lump of clay just as we are. So if the pastor has said something wrong to you or done something in the church that you think is wrong, you should go to him and talk to him about it as opposed to going behind his back and talking about him with another church member. But you can't allow that to get in the way of you receiving the Word. If a child comes to you with a word of wisdom, will you refuse it because it's coming from a child and in your mind you should always teach the child as opposed to the other way around? If you do, then you're foolish to do so. We must be willing to accept wisdom in what ever package God delivers it in. And that includes a minister that you may or may not think is living right.

We have begun to go to church for all of the wrong reasons. Just as a lot of us have began to crowd the churches where pastors are preaching prosperity in hopes that we can eat of the fruit that falls from the prosperity tree, we also go to church to gossip, we go for "blessings", we go to date and some of us go just to complain about what's going on. We also go to spread rumors about the pastor and about other members of the church. All reasons that fall short of why we *should* be there. There are many reasons we do these things, but the main reason that one wishes to bring down another is because of their own shortcomings.

When we're miserable, we sometimes attempt to project our misery onto others instead of correcting our own situation.

This is the main reason that so many people are turned off by traditional church values and turned on by churches of prosperity. When they look into a traditional church that supposedly has traditional values, they feel like they're looking into a mirror. They see no difference between us and them. We talk about God and His goodness, but we still share similarities with them. We share the same vices and we seem just as miserable as they are living in the secular world. Is it different in the prosperity churches? No, it isn't. Those people seem even more crooked to the secular world, but because they have more material possessions, they seem happier. So even in the face of hypocrisy, backbiting, gossiping, fornication, adultery and judgmental people that exists in <u>all</u> churches, those in the secular world will go where the money is.

Now, I'm not suggesting that one should stay where they aren't happy. I said earlier that God doesn't want us to serve in misery. What I am saying is that if you feel so strongly that your pastor isn't right, then why keep coming back to that church? Why risk speaking against one of God's chosen? Instead of gossiping, why not move your membership? As I also said earlier, there's more than one pastor out here that can help you see the Kingdom of God. We're all humans and sometimes we don't get along. Don't poison the congregation, because God will hold you accountable. I've found that church is more enjoyable when you go for the right reasons as opposed to getting caught up in individual behaviors, cliques and things that don't concern worshiping God. If you're unhappy in your current church situation, find somewhere else to worship and get on with the business of getting yourself saved.

<u>*The People's Court*</u>

I talked earlier about certain radio hosts, authors and ministers that I've heard speak out about the prosperity preachers and call themselves taking them to task or calling them out. The traditional thinking is that if a man of God is not living right, not only will God deal with him in His own way, He will deal with him much more severely than He will us because that preacher has been misusing his status and misleading the people. I still believe in that philosophy. We aren't here to sit in judgment of God's preachers. But others seem to think that we should just call them out, sometimes publicly, and not wait for God to handle His own business. A phrase about glass houses and stones has immediately come to my mind.

If I take it upon myself to "expose" those that I think are doing wrong, how long will it be before someone "exposes" me? We have to be careful because sometimes people may be doing wrong and sometimes our information is suspect because it's coming from someone with an axe to grind. Are some of these people that are "exposing" these preachers really reacting from the heart because they think that something's not right? Yes. Are some of these people just jealous of that minister, his status and his possessions? Yes. Are some of these people being mislead by others from within that particular congregation with the aforementioned axe to grind? Absolutely. But there's something wrong with all of us and I don't know about you, but I'd like my demons to be exercised by me and my God with no involvement from the general public.

I said in my first book that we shouldn't do things that we'd be ashamed of if someone found out about them and that would eliminate the desire to tell one another lies. Any preacher should follow that code, and if you do become exposed for your wrongdoings, then that's the chance you took when you decided to do wrong. But the problem with us as a society is that we feel that it's always up to us to dispense justice upon an individual. In the case of the laws of the land, that may be true. But theocratic matters should be left to God. We get so caught up in making sure that someone pays for what we deem wrong that we become judge, jury and executioner.

We're sometimes not willing to wait for God to take care of His business. That's why we have capital punishment in this country. We're so afraid that He won't do it as quickly as we'd like or to our satisfaction that we just jump right in and make sure that justice is served, never giving a thought to the fact that we could be wrong. In fact, there's even word going around that this God will actually forgive those who have done wrong as long as they truly repent and seek His forgiveness. Are you kidding me? We can't have any of that, can we? We as "Christians" aren't gonna stand for that, are we? If God is willing to forgive that killer, that rapist or that drug dealer, then what are we to do? We can't let Him go soft on the issues, so we may as well kill these people ourselves.

But what if we were given misinformation or we were wrong about what we saw? What if we have publicly brought shame on someone who had done no wrong? We all know how public perceptions can be and how hard they can be to live down. But once the damage is done, we sometimes can't reverse that. That's why we need to let God handle His preachers. I'm 100% sure that He not only knows for sure what's been done right or wrong, but His punishment will be just and fair.

As for the prosperity preachers that face such scrutiny and skepticism, the only thing I can say is you knew what the job was about when you took it. You can't even tell people that you're saved without instantly being judged, so if you say you're a preacher, you get it from all sides. If you know the Word of God, then you know what's bound to happen. Just look at all the examples that I gave earlier that existed throughout the Bible. I'm sure that preachers back in those times were criticized if their camel was better than the others or they had the nicest hut in the village.

All jokes aside, we as Christians have to be willing to admit that some criticism of us is fair. Some of these preachers do dress like pimps, and no matter what message you're preaching, I don't know if that should be. A nice, modest suit should be good enough. Do we really need the bright red gators and the long chain with cross on the end? Sometimes it does look like a rap video is about to break out.

As for the cars, the houses and the private jets, I will admit that I think it's a tad bit overboard. If you're doing missionary work all over the world, maybe the jet is necessary. But I've told people that I know that I don't think a Bentley makes sense for anyone. Whether you're a preacher, a rapper, an entertainer or whatever. Is there ever really a NEED for a car that cost between a quarter of a million dollars and a half million dollars? No matter what you do for a living, in my mind, the answer is no. Should you get one if you can afford it? It's your money, so I guess you can, but it never has and never will make sense to me. As a minister, even if you've done a ton of work for those less fortunate, there's always something more that can be done. Putting that kind of money into a car when people still sleep on the ground somewhere in this country doesn't make sense. At least a house can maintain or increase in value, and the land can be passed on from generation to generation. You can't save the world all by yourself, but if you're a man of God, you should never stop trying. We should all never stop trying.

When you make those kinds of statements, people think that you want the preacher to live like a poor man. They think that you don't want God's preacher to have anything. That's not what I'm saying, but some things are excessive to me. If my pastor is a pastor on Sunday and a lawyer through the week, then this would make more sense. If he's writing books, or he's a doctor or doing something else to bring in that kind of income, then this makes more sense. I don't know if a church should ever buy a pastor a car that costs that much. It's just my opinion. If he has to have a car that costs that much, he should buy it on his on.

Once you bring business into the church at the expense of Jesus Christ, you run the risk of things like this happening. When people are bringing their tithes into the storehouse and all their getting is a message about prosperity, they will trip when they don't appear to be as prosperous as you are. And you can't just look at them and say "Pray harder". If all of the messages are about money, then your people will want money. That becomes their focal point. Not salvation, not getting to the Kingdom, not treating each other right, not the marriage of the mental, spiritual and the flesh and not the fact that whatever they amass here on earth will still be here on earth when they die. If you feed them a message of money, then that's all they'll look forward to. And if they don't achieve it to your level or the level of their fellow church members, they'll still be miserable and they will cast aspersions upon you.

Business and a sense of business belong in the church. As I said before, if you don't run your church as a business, it will fail. Teaching the church members about money and being prosperous is also necessary, especially in the black community. We don't always have a proper understanding of money and how it works and I can't think of a better place to learn about all aspects of life than in your place of worship so that it can be tied in with God and His Word. Money has been a subject of taboo in the church for years. As I said earlier, members have often rolled their eyes whenever the collection plate was brought out. Why do we need so many offerings? You don't appreciate that benevolent offering until you're in need. Why do we sometimes take a special offering? Because every time the church doors open, there's a cost. Lights, gas, water and such aren't free, not even to the church. The church has expenses and it isn't just up to the pastor to take care of them. It's our church, so it's our responsibility.

Some of our larger churches tend to attract more prosperous members. These doctors, lawyers, bankers, real estate agents, etc. can teach us all a thing or two. It gives us an opportunity to pool our resources and help one another out. This is where we should look for our opportunities at prosperity. Though our pastor can offer us guidance in the way of being prosperous, his *primary* focus should be to give you spiritual guidance. He should be about your spiritual prosperity. Every preacher that leads one of these churches isn't living wrong just because he drives a nice car or lives in a nice neighborhood. Just because thousands of people are hanging on his every word doesn't mean that he's getting over on someone. God has sent some of these ministers here to lead thousands to Him.

As I said before, I do believe in some of these ministers. As much as I'd like to name them, I won't here because by naming them I may in effect be suggesting that those that I didn't name are people I suspect of not living right. Just like those of you reading this, I have two lists going. But also, as I said before, God is working with me on that just as He is with you. I don't want to sit in judgment of those that preach only about prosperity. I simply want Jesus to make His way back to the forefront of whatever we preach about. He should always be the centerpiece.

I also want to be something different than those that I spoke about who would use their platform to attack individuals and name names as opposed to attacking the issues. They seem to be asking "Who do these preachers think they are telling me to live right when it's clear by the wheels of their Bentleys and by the blades of grass on their acres and acres of property that they're living afoul of God's law?" They seem to be wondering how these ministers can go around claiming to be about God when they can clearly see that they're not. They seem to holding two hands full of stones while their skeletons lie neatly tucked away in their closets. Sometimes the hardest advice to follow is your own. Judge not, lest ye be judged.

Chapter 5

Time's a wastin': Will it take tragedy for you to re-order your steps?

Just as a lot of us tend to do when we reach that "death sentence" called 30, we tend to become just as reflective about life as I have in my work. We tend to recall some of the seemingly smallest events of our lives with great reverence. As I continue to get older, I feel that I'm experiencing a brand new growth each day. I can honestly say that I've never had some of the "bad habits" that others have had in their lives. I've never had a drink in my life and I've never smoked. The amount of real partying that I've done in my life is miniscule compared to even the prudish among us. Yes, I was always quiet and somewhat to myself. At the same time, I was nowhere near perfect. If I ever had a vice, it was women, as my oldest brother correctly predicted would be the case many, many years ago. If I were Superman, they'd surely be my kryptonite. That and Mountain Dew. But sometimes, God has a greater plan for us than those vices that hold us back so often. Sometimes it takes us a while to see it and accept it, and sometimes we have to go through some things to become more aware of it. But for each individual, God has a plan for greatness. We just have to be ready when that opportunity presents itself, grab hold of it, and never let go.

During the writing of this book and my first one, *Temporarily Disconnected*, I feel that I've gotten myself in touch with what God wants me to do. I've accomplished a lot of things in my life for someone that has never spent a day in college. Granted, I have had some form of higher education. I was raised in God's house, and there can be no higher form of education than that. But I also went to broadcast school after high school (eventually). But I guess I'm just one of those people that was supposed to make something out of himself whether they went to college or not. But even with my successes in life, I still feel that I've wasted part of my life on frivolous things. I've always been quite the procrastinator and there were plenty of times during my twenties that I could've been doing way more productive things with myself. I've had opportunities that have slipped through my fingers due to my own unwillingness to work harder at a given project or two.

I've also wasted plenty of emotional time in my life. I've been involved in relationships with people that were not only unproductive, but they were also quite damaging to my views on the opposite gender. Now, I'm not headed to the studio to record my version of (insert misogynistic rap song title here) to express my anger with the ladies. That's not what I'm saying. Although, if you read *Temporarily Disconnected*, you know that I feel that some of you ladies are responsible for some of the young men of today calling you (insert derogatory name for female here) on a regular basis. But what I am saying is that I am a lot more cautious about the women that I get involved with because of some bad experiences I've had. More than that, I've noticed that I've become somewhat emotionally unavailable to love. After you've been hurt a couple of times, things tend to get that way.

If you've ever been there, then you know what I'm talking about. We can spend a lot of time with people in our lives that are undeserving of such attention. Sometimes in the name of love, and most times in the name of lust. We become unavailable to some real possibilities in our romantic lives because we're holding on to some things that don't make sense. So often, we become comfortable with where we are and what we supposedly have with another person. We either convince ourselves that we're in a fruitful relationship, that there's nothing wrong with what's going on or in some cases, we may actually convince ourselves that we can do no better. At any rate, you can waste a lot of time and a lot of emotion on people that have little or nothing to bring you other than conversation and a pointless roll in the hay. Although good conversation is nice, it's the pointless roll in the hay that you should be concerned about.

We have to be careful of the love that we willingly give out to, and sometimes waste on certain individuals. It's something that I touched on in my first book. You'd hate to wake up 10 years after the fact and find out that you've wasted time, years, and more importantly, love that you'll never get back, on an individual that was just not worth the trouble. Life is simply too short for that. We do a lot of wasteful things in our lives because we're always under the impression that we have time to correct the mistakes of our youth and ignorance.

Without sounding too Armageddon or doom and gloom, none of us are promised tomorrow. The old saying that you shouldn't put off 'til tomorrow what you could do today doesn't just apply to starting things that we may have put off due to procrastination. It also applies to ending some things in our lives that have become unproductive. That saying is a call to action. It's up to us to determine what action is necessary in our individual lives. Eliminating wasteful attitudes and behaviors in our lives is most times a tall order, that's for sure. Especially when you consider the fact that a lot of us have spent so much time living that way. But that journey must begin with that first step.

We may never get to that point in our lives where every moment in life is lived with some sort of purpose behind it, and I don't know if one ever should. When I speak of the need for us to make better use of our time and our lives, I'm not suggesting an all work, no play life. In fact, I'm totally against that. What I *am* in favor of is not being as wasteful as we have been with our lives. I *am* talking about not focusing so much on things that don't really matter in this life. We sometimes become so arrogant that we don't realize that time is slipping away each day. It's come to the point that tragedy has to strike within our lives before we even remember how important family is supposed to be in our lives (I'll touch on that near the end of this chapter).

Make no mistake about it though, I'm not writing this book as a person that has somehow figured this out. I'm still struggling everyday to eliminate some things from my life that make no sense, both on the professional side and the personal side of my life. I don't ever want anybody to feel as if I'm speaking as a guy who's figured it out. Instead, I want people to be able to read the words of someone stuck in the struggle just like they are. There are too many books in circulation from people who have "figured it out", and want to tell you how to get yourself together. I'm coming from a different place. I'm not in the penthouse, I'm still in the 'hood. I'm trying to figure out this thing called life just like you are.

An idle mind...

As I said when I opened this Chapter, the process of getting older (and hopefully wiser), usually causes us to become a bit more reflective. It causes us to think back on some of the things that we have, or in some cases haven't done in and with our lives. So, I've had to ask myself some questions that maybe some of you have asked yourself: Have I done all that I can with all of the ability that God has given me? Have I lived each day to the fullest or have I let precious time just slip away while I did nothing? Have I wasted emotional time on and with people that weren't worthy of such commitment from me? And most of all, if I've experienced a less than fulfilling life both emotionally and spiritually, how much of it is just the way things go sometimes, and how much of it is all my fault? While some questions in our lives will sometimes go unanswered, others demand a response. At this point in my life, I'm becoming more demanding of myself.

I feel that all of us are born with certain abilities. Now, when I speak of abilities, we mustn't confuse having ability with possessing special talents. Having ability just means that you're able to do any number of things reasonably well. Having a special talent for something means that you're probably able to do something very unique that very few others are able to do. For example, some people can sing, while others may be good at sewing. Some are good at sports, while others are good at retail management. Some are good at teaching and motivating others, while others may be good at gardening.

There are a thousand different examples that I could give. While we all enjoy a good movie staring our favorite actor or actress, what good would Denzel do you if you needed a plumber, ASAP? While we all enjoy a good song by our favorite singer, rapper or band from time to time, one can't really put a price on knowing a good, reliable and fair mechanic, and I don't think a Jay-Z, a Kanye West or a Beyonce would fit the bill. And although it's nice to watch Shaq dominate a game or Ben Wallace block shots and dunk on the break in all of his afro glory, if you've ever had any electrical issues in your home, you know how invaluable a good electrician can be. And though these brothers can electrify a crowd, I don't know how far they'd get trying to electrify your house. The bottom line is, no matter how great your gift may appear to be or how minor your talent seems, we've all been blessed with the ability to make someone's life better.

However, finding that ability can sometimes be a completely different story. As I said before, we sometimes confuse ability with being gifted. When this happens, the results can sometimes be disastrous. Not only can you waste a lot of time doing things that you're no good at, you could subject some of us in the general population to some of your attempts at greatness. Now, before some of you get all huffy and think that I'm being mean, hear me out. If you've ever sat in church and listened to Sister or Brother So-and-So singing that song during devotional service and wondered to yourself how you could disconnect the PA system without anyone noticing, you know exactly what I'm talking about. On the one hand, it doesn't matter how you sound when you're praising the Lord. If you're singing His praises, it's a beautiful sound. In theory. On the other hand, we sometimes don't have the heart to tell people that it may be time to pick up an instrument and keep silent.

Better yet, how many times have you allowed your best friend's girlfriend's cousin on her daddy's side to work on your car, only to get it back in worse condition than it was when you gave it to him? Is there any wonder this dude doesn't have a regular gig is somebody's garage? Sure, we all know a few 'hood mechanics and if you know a good one, he can save you a lot of dough. But if you mess around and let his boy, who's nowhere near as good as he is and is only good for handing wrenches to real mechanics, get under your hood and start connecting and disconnecting things, you could be at the dealership sooner than you think.

Without boring you with any more analogies, we all have either gifts or abilities that we've been blessed with. With that said, there are a lot of different reasons that we may fall short of what we're supposed to be in life. Continuing with what I've talked about in the last couple of paragraphs, one of the most glaring ways in which we do this is by believing that we're capable of things that we just aren't capable of. Believing that you could be a singer when you can't carry a tune, believing that you're a mechanic because you used to hang around with mechanics, believing that you're NBA bound because you dominated the game in Jr. High, believing you can write books because you can string a few words together and make sentences (wait, that's me!) or thinking you can cook because *you* can stand the taste of your own food. We must be realistic about our capabilities. Knowing and understanding your potential and your abilities is very important, but it actually may be more important to know your limitations.

I've been writing since I was in high school. The first poem I ever wrote was about a girl in one of my classes that I had a crush on. I don't remember her name and she never saw a word of what

I wrote because I never had the nerve to even speak to her, much less approach her about my "feelings". In fact, I was so afraid, I still have that poem. That was the first time I was aware that I might have a talent for writing. I never got a date, but my crush led to me realizing that I had a talent, and from there, I began writing more poems.

One after the other, they got better and better. I was pretty good for a high school kid. Soon after that, my mom found out I was writing. She found this big black notebook that I kept my poems in and she just went right ahead and started reading through it. She later told me that she thought it was a phonebook, but come on. I mean, I was a handsome young man, but my mom thinking I needed a full-sized notebook to keep up with all of my phone numbers? My being a playa like that was at least one to two years away, my goodness. All jokes aside, what my mom saw was my potential. Now, maybe she was just being a supportive mom, but she wanted to support what she saw as a gift. She urged me to continue my writing so that I could publish my works one day.

At this point in my life, I had spent 3 years in the high school orchestra as a First Chair Cellist. With my ability to write and my talents in music, you could see that my mom probably felt that she had a pretty talented child on her hands. The writing was just something that I picked up and saw as a hobby. My father was a musician, so, to me, the music and the love that I have for it was in my veins. Although I hated being in the orchestra, the cello was so easy for me to play. In a black high school in the 'hood, you couldn't be more lame than to be in the orchestra, but I did it because my mom liked the fact that I was in there.

The instrument came so easy to me that I never practiced at all and I was still good. My father was a guitarist, so I guess all of the finger positions were just natural. But that also came to be a curse on me. Because everything came so easy, I never felt the need to work at it. It drove my conductor crazy because she could see my potential. For example, she wanted me to go away for two weeks one summer to a music camp. Because she knew so many people in the high school music community in the state, she knew that I was one of the best cellists in the state. But being young, immature and unable to see the opportunity in front of me, there was no way that I was giving up any part of my summer for some snobbish music camp. Although one could understand why a young mind couldn't see that opportunity, it was still a poor decision on my part and I did eventually regret it.

I never embraced the talent that I possessed because it just didn't seem cool to me. I mean, I was raised on hip hop music. Who plays a cello in hip hop? Besides, if I ever had dreams of playing anything, it was a guitar. I wanted to be able to play like Prince. That was cool to me. That's how I wound up in the orchestra in the first place. It was supposed to be a strings class and my counselor told me that they could teach me to play guitar. My counselor was a liar. Okay, maybe not a liar, but as a guidance counselor, she was misguiding me on that day.

Anyway, because I was so naive, I couldn't see that my musical heroes like Prince and Michael Jackson had great reverence for all forms of music. Even though I have always listened to all forms of music, I never could touch classical. It just bored the hell out of me, and in my young mind, I thought that classical music would be the only place that I could find a cello. It wasn't until I was able to buy my own music and started reading liner notes that I realized how wrong I was.

Just like it was with so very much that I've learned about music in my life, it was Prince that opened my eyes. The way one listens to music as just a lover of music and as a musician is totally different. When you just listen to music because you enjoy it, more times than not, you just hear the sounds of beautiful music. You're not really interested in what makes this sound or that sound, you just know you like the song. When you listen as a musician, you hear something completely different.

All of those subtle nuances that make up a great song that were supposedly hidden beneath the surface are now blaring loudly in your ears. You hear the difference between a real piano and an electric one. You hear the difference between real drums and electronic drums or a drum machine. You learn your bass parts, guitar parts, your different rhythms and harmonies and so on. You become much more aware of all of the individual parts of a song, what they bring to the song and how they all come together to make one great composition.

What I begin to hear in Prince's music was that he started incorporating real strings, rather than synthesized strings, into his music. For example, at the very end of the song "Purple Rain", I heard some very, very familiar sounds. It was the sound of cellos and violins and such. I couldn't believe that one of my musical heroes would incorporate those "lame" strings into his music, and yet somehow, he did it so beautifully. It continued on his next album and it's still there today in his music whenever he sees fit.

So, from there, I realized a couple of things. First, what you do, or in this case, what you play, doesn't make you who you are. Second, had I realized that first thing and taken my craft more seriously, it could've taken me many places, maybe even a recording studio to record with and for a legend. It's easier to rebound from such shortsightedness when it happens in your youth. Just do your best to make sure that it doesn't carry over into your adult years.

In my senior year, I "retired" from the orchestra and just sought to finish high school. Still unsure of what I wanted to do with myself, I began to write a lot more. I was finally taking it seriously. So much that I became very protective about what I was writing. I wrote only poetry and short stories, but I really started to realize that I could be good with words. My mother was still pushing me to publish my works, but I was still not committed enough to do it. She saw my potential and like the wonderful mother that she is, she wanted me to reach it. But just like my days as a cellist, it was all too easy to me.

Poetry came to me so naturally, that I could write one on the spot. For example, one night I was at my girlfriend's house. It was Valentine's Day, and I had given her a poem with her flowers. She thought it would be a nice gesture if I could give her mom a poem one day because her mother loved poetry. I told her that if she felt that way, then I'd write one right then and there. She told me that her mom would be home from work in the next 5 minutes, so I should just wait until I had more time to write one. I told her that if she was giving me 5 minutes, that was 2 more than I needed.

With that, I took a pen and a pad and wrote a poem for her mom and delivered it as soon as she walked in the door. It came so easy, that sometimes I questioned how good they may actually be because I could write them so frequently. But just like your Batmen, your Spider Men and your Supermen of the world, with great power (or in this case, talent), comes great responsibility.

The Bible says to whom much is given, much is required (Luke 12:48). My responsibility to my talents and to God, who gave me those talents, was to appreciate them and to work hard at them. Although I cared a lot about my writing, I didn't always show the right appreciation for my gift. Until now.

The point of me telling all of these stories of my youth is to point out the fact that we can be given so much in our lives in the way of talent and/or ability, but if you don't take advantage of it, you may go on to live a life unfulfilled. As I'm writing this book now, I feel that I'm living out a prophecy. I was destined to be more than I've been so far in my life and if no one reads my works but my immediate family and my friends, I will still feel a sense of accomplishment. When you have been blessed with a particular talent or ability, you have to be willing to share your gift with the world. You never know how you may impact another's life through your works.

A friend of mine once told me that because of something I said to her when we were teenagers, she changed her life. She told me that if it weren't for me and my family, she'd be dead because of some of the things she was involved in and because of the way she was living. I don't think that's totally true. If it weren't for God, she'd be dead. I don't think any of us have the ability to save a life without God being involved, but we can say or do things that can inspire others to do great things. We can say or do things that inspire others to change.

Maybe that's my gift. I'm not sure, as I just told her what I thought she needed to hear. I have always been one to speak my mind and say what I feel, and I'm sure I was just doing that at the time. Although neither of us can say for sure what would've happened had I not said whatever it is that I said, with her revealing her point of view to me, I can't help but wonder what would've happened had I not spoken up. Fortunately, God was working through me that day and I didn't lose another friend to the streets.

<u>*No more government aide*</u>

The time has come for all of us to look inside of ourselves and ask some tough questions. There has to be more to one's life than all of the materialistic and carnal things that we find ourselves so wrapped up in these days. When I started writing this book, we were 3 ½ to 4 years removed from the 9/11 tragedy. When those Towers fell, the whole country seemed to be wrapped up in this new spirit of togetherness. We had all vowed to become better people and to treat one another better. We had all decided that we were going to live for the moment and not wait 'til tomorrow to do all of the things that we're supposed to be doing in our lives today.

We all vowed to put our families first and take time out for the things in life that really matter. We were supposedly going to go forward to a brand new day in this country. There was supposed to be a new feeling of brotherhood all throughout this land. Blacks and whites were getting along, cats and dogs were living together in harmony, and so on and so forth. With the exception of all our price gouging brethren at the, uh, local filling stations, we were supposedly on some sort of peace train. How soon we forget, or in that case, forgot. Peace train derailed.

Before I finished this book, we were faced with another disaster in this country. However, the results of this one were very, very different. This time, it wasn't a foe that we could blame for our going off and starting unnecessary wars that we were facing. This time, it was something that we really couldn't do anything about. So-called Mother Nature took her toll on the southern part of this country. This particular disaster was natural in its form. Hurricane Katrina was the most devastating natural disaster that I've seen in this country in my lifetime. Practically the entire city of New Orleans was submerged under water. I never thought I'd ever see the day that I would see rows and rows of homes completely under water. The city had *become* the sea. However, when this disaster hit, there wasn't the same camaraderie that existed when the Towers were hit. As strange as it seems, the so-called greatest nation on the planet reacted differently this time.

When those Towers fell in New York, everybody in this country and in our government took just about every resource we could spare and sent them to the city that never sleeps. Just the thought of someone coming onto American soil and killing that many of our citizens brought about a myriad of emotions in all Americans. There was enough frustration and anger to go around twice, but more than anything, there was compassion. There was compassion for the victims in the planes that crashed into the Towers, those who weren't able to escape the Towers, and all of the family members that they left behind. All of America felt a sense of loss, whether you lost a loved one in this tragedy or not.

I remember not being able to sleep nights just thinking about all of the bodies trapped beneath that rubble in New York. In July of 2007, my family reunion was held in Newark, NJ and I was able to visit New York for the first time in my life. I was able to see Ground Zero first hand. Though it had been almost 6 years since the tragedy, there was still a giant hole in the ground where those buildings used to be. It was all I could do to fight back my tears as I was instantly transported back to that day in September 2001.

I was also reminded of how jaded we can be as a society, as a place of death and devastation is now somewhat of a tourist attraction, complete with jackasses waiting to sell us pictures of the Towers falling as we got off of the bus to see the ruins. Maybe I'm being a bit melodramatic, but I thought I saw a few too many smiling faces there. Although I'm sure that a lot has been changed, cleaned up and such, I was still able to photograph what appeared to be rubble. Rubble from 6 years prior. We should all feel blessed that we're still alive in the wake of such events even being possible here on earth, but you can forgive me if I didn't feel like smiling that day.

In some ways, our country lay in ruins on that day in September of 2001. We all felt as if we had lost something. The very thing that our nation was supposedly built on was being threatened. Someone was threatening to take away our freedom. Our whole way of life changed for a few weeks. It became an adventure just to go to the local gas station because so many of them were owned by people from foreign lands. Within our newfound sense of brotherhood, we had begun to practice hatred and racial profiling of a different kind. If someone even looked to be of Middle Eastern descent, we immediately became skeptical of them.

This was something that our government not only condoned in many ways, they practiced it themselves. As police began to round up foreigners one by one in an attempt to restore order, I must admit that I felt no sympathy. Being a black man and having watched my people being victimized by the government all of my life simply for being black, I noticed how strange all of this seemed. In my mind, I was thinking that all of this time, I could be pulled over simply for being black and in the wrong neighborhood. I could be beaten for simply dating a white woman. Myself, and others like me, could be denied housing in certain neighborhoods just because someone couldn't bear having black folks as neighbors.

This country was so worried about people who fought along side them for the very freedoms that we all possess, that it couldn't see some things that were real dangers to them. No matter what this country may have thought of my people, we had never done anything this heinous. Sure, we've sold drugs, but they we're drugs provided by and sold for white men. No matter what they thought about blacks, we would've never blown up buildings, killing thousands and crippling our own economy. While they spent precious time and energy watching me and my buddies, they allowed people who really sought to do us harm to come into our country illegally, live here for years and learn to fly in our flight schools, all for the sole purpose of getting on our planes, crashing into our buildings and crippling our economy. Is this country great or what?

One might suggest that America's heart was in the right place all along. (Sarcasm alert) Sure, we may have overreacted when we started jailing anyone that looked like there were from Afghanistan, but we were simply trying to take care of home. I mean, this is the USA, dammit. We don't stand for that kind of thing 'round here. We take care of our own and when something comes along and hurts our people in mass the way that the terrorists did, we take action. However, what we learned from the next disaster is that it depends on what happens to what people in which part of the country that will determine how our government reacts.

As I said earlier, when the Towers fell, we all felt the need to respond, and respond swiftly. However, when Katrina came ashore, our government was no longer willing to throw caution to the wind in an effort to save their fellow man. All of a sudden, a harsh reality was brought to the forefront once again. That feeling of togetherness had long since worn off. What had become joined together through tragedy had been torn apart again through complacency. Slowly, but surely, America had become separate again. The haves on one side, and the have-nots on the other. When this tragedy came ashore, America went from swiftly to shifty in a heartbeat. Sometimes, all it takes is a tragedy to show us how close we can become or how far apart we really are. Need an example? Just as something like the falling of those Towers can make blacks and whites stand together for seemingly one common cause, the O.J. Trial and the Rodney King verdict showed us just how far apart the races still are in this country.

For a week or two before it hit land, Hurricane Katrina was predicted to do significant damage. That promise was kept in a major way. When she finally came through and devastated the south, a lot of people lost everything. Not the "everything" we feel like we lose when some relationship is lost, I'm talking about EVERYTHING! All of their possessions, and in some cases, all of their families. Complete homes were washed away, and entire families we displaced, separated or lost in the flood altogether. Once again, it was time for our country to come together. Just like it was when the Towers fell, we were supposed to pool our resources and send what we could while our government stepped up and saved as many as they could, as quickly as they could.

Instead, what we found out was this ain't September 2001 and we ain't in New York no more. When our government was faced with the opportunity to prove that this really is the land of the free, home of the brave and that all men truly are equal, what they wound up proving was something that most blacks this side of Kanye West (who famously and accurately stated on a live Hurricane Katrina benefit broadcast, "George Bush doesn't like black people") already knew: There always has been and always will be a division between blacks and whites, blacks and government and rich and poor in this country.

When a disaster happens in this country and it affects that very small group of people that can actually call themselves rich, our government sprints into action. Sure, what happened in New York affected the pockets of all Americans. But the implication was that it was an attack on one of the so-called greatest city in the world and an attack on our economy. Pretty much everyone's money flowed through New York's financial district, so when young Osama came through and crushed the buildings like Snoop Dogg in the "New York, New York" video, we had to do something.

You can't just come in here and take down the ole US of A that way. We're not even gonna think about what happened, we're just gonna go in and get to work. But when Katrina came through and did her thing in the south, we had to react with caution. We had to assess the damage before we just rushed right in. Could it be that our beloved government reacted differently because of where these two disasters happened and who was affected by each of them? What do you think?

If it seems that I'm accusing our government of reacting slowly because most of the people in the south that were affected by the hurricane were black, well, that's only partially true. Although I do believe that, in large part, it had a lot to do with the fact that the majority of the people that were affected were black, it had more to do with the fact that they were poor. The government's neglect had more to do with class than anything else. If the Hurricane had gone through, say, The Hamptons, there would've been trips made every 15 minutes to get those people out of there. In fact, when hurricanes swept through Jeb Bush country down in Florida, things were taken care of quick, fast and in a hurry. Isn't that odd? Am I to believe that the citizens of Florida and New York are somehow better than the citizens of New Orleans and Mississippi? If actions speak louder than words, then I guess that's what George "Dubya" and the boys were saying.

Now that they're engaged, I'm about to marry these two tragic events in American history. When pressed about why it took them so long to respond to the devastation in the south, our government told us that they were trying as hard as they could, but even in the so-called greatest country on earth, there was only so much they could do because their resources were limited. And they were right. But how can the resources be limited in such a great country, you ask? Why weren't the resources limited 4 years prior, under circumstances much more dangerous?

Not just because the government is prejudice against race *and* the lower class, oh no. It's because our government didn't have so many resources tied up in an unjust war in 2001. Yes, our resources are limited because we're so busy supposedly trying to save some other country, (a country that doesn't even want us there, mind you), when we can't even save ourselves. The kicker in all of this is the fact that some of us understood that we did have limited resources in this situation. The things that we weren't able to get over were the reason our resources were so limited (greed, the pursuit of oil, the aforementioned unjust war), and the slow response with the resources that we actually *did* have. I mean, if CNN can get a helicopter over the city so that they could report that the black people were "looting" and the white people were "looking for food so that they can survive and feed their families (like blacks don't have families to feed; contrary to popular belief, the black family does still exist)", then surely our government is more powerful than CNN, right?

Now, I'm sure it seems that I went on a rant for a few pages, but I swear, I'll tie this up like a 5 year old ties knots in his shoelaces. Just like it was with 9/11, this disaster should have made us all aware of what we really have in this life and what's really important. If you have a soul at all, you should be changed by what you saw. This shouldn't be something that causes only the directly affected to be changed. We should all be directly affected.

When those Towers fell and when Katrina hit, they didn't care about black or white. Neither cared who was fat or skinny. Neither cared who drove a Hyundai and who drove a Yukon Denali with 24-inch rims on it. The Towers fell, no matter what your status was. The hurricane hit, no matter how fine you were. When you're scrambling to save your life, who really cares about such things? And when you look around for a loved one missing, who cares about how much money you have? Ask yourself, would it take all that you have floating away from you for you to realize what's really important in your life? Would you have to have everything taken away from you in order to understand what you really need to survive in this life?

Through tragedy's tears, we can be new

One day I was watching Oprah (yes, I said Oprah), and she said something concerning Hurricane Katrina that I found very poignant. She said, when speaking to a hurricane survivor that had lost everything, the woman said to her, "Once I lost everything, that's when I realized that I could survive with nothing". That struck a chord with me because I've long since wondered why we trick ourselves into believing that we can't survive without some things in our lives. All of the material possessions in the world didn't amount to a hill of beans once these disasters took place.

Why do we, especially us as blacks, always have to lose so much in order realize what's important? Now, I'm not saying that the people of New Orleans and Mississippi were living the high life before all of this drama unfolded, but when disaster strikes and affects that many blacks at one time, we all usually feel that pain. We all become more reflective for a short period of time. We all seem to think that we understand what life should be about. But before you can blink an eye, we're back to wasting our lives and living beyond our means, all to impress people who probably wouldn't care about us otherwise.

When things like this happen to others and we as a people have to watch it on TV, we always have the option of turning the channel or turning the TV off altogether. Sometimes it's an escape that we're looking for. Sometimes we just can't take anymore. That's totally understandable. The problem with that is, out of sight, out of mind. We tend to forget what's going on as long as we can't see it. We don't think about those people that can't turn any of this off or change the channel.

What makes the Katrina situation so disturbing is that it couldn't have happened to a more fragile set of people. A lot of these people were barely hanging on as it is. The last thing that they could afford to have happen was for some out of control weather system to come along and destroy all that they had. These are the people that can least afford to lose anything because they have no real resources to look to in the way of rebuilding. I mean, when you think about it, a lot of those people in New Orleans lost all of their possessions *and* their jobs, all at once. How soon can one relocate and rebuild in that situation? With that being said, when I think about how ungrateful we have become as a society, it just makes a situation like this seem that much more unbearable.

God has truly blessed so many of us with the talents that I've mentioned, with wealth and with health. Yet, so many of us are selfish, lazy and won't do anything for anyone unless we feel that we can be compensated somehow for it. I once wrote a poem to a friend to express some regret that I was feeling over the fact that we weren't speaking. In the wake of Katrina, I told her that I was one natural disaster away from never speaking again. My point to her was that we never know what we make wake up to tomorrow. In fact, we never know if we *will* wake up tomorrow at all.

Life wasn't meant to be filled with regret. If you don't get all that you can out of life, you will be filled with regret. So often, when one thinks of getting the most out of life, we think of things in a worldly since. Travel, material things, physical pleasures and so on. Although those things are a part of life and should be experienced in moderation, I keep waiting for the day that we began to get the most out of our spiritual lives as well. I keep waiting for the day that we realize that whether or not we're properly utilizing our time on this earth, time continues on. Unless tragedy strikes, those of us who are young will become old. It should be upon all of us to get the most out of our gifts and abilities simply because we have been blessed, rather than waiting for our own personal Katrina or 9/11 to come along before we realize what we should be doing with our lives.

If it seems that I'm speaking in dire terms, then you're reading this right. Wasting time working jobs that are unfulfilling, wasting emotional time with people in unfruitful relationships and wasting day after day doing absolutely nothing with your life are things that we must put behind us. I was blessed not to have lost anyone close to me in either of the tragedies that I've spoken on, but they definitely got my attention.

Through those tragedies I was able to see that I've wasted certain parts of my life. Now, my life hasn't been a total waste as I have accomplished some things, but as I said before, there were certainly some things that I could've either done better or worked harder at. And that includes both my personal and professional lives. I have always thought of myself as a decent and enlightened person. That part, I felt like I had down. But we could all be doing more. We could all be doing better.

I've decided to stop talking about change, and be about change. These days, my outlet has become expressing myself through my writing. Through these pages, I hope to inspire some, uplift others, educate a few and cause many to reflect. I believe that's my gift from God and it's my duty to share it with the world. I've decided not to let tragedy dictate when I should search my soul for a better me. I've decided that I should search myself daily for that. No explosions, plane crashes or hurricanes necessary. I just wanna be sure that my life has meaning and purpose at all times. As I'm making this promise, I know that God is listening to every word I'm saying. I know He hasn't always been pleased at what I've been. I just hope that He's pleased at what I'm becoming.

Chapter 6

What would Jesus do?

I'm sure we're all familiar with that phrase, right? "What would Jesus do?" You could check the wrist of the person sitting next to you right now, check the license plate of the car in front of you the next time you're driving (because I certainly hope you're not reading this book while driving) or read the t-shirt of the nearest Christian you can find. Chances are you'll see those words or these letters: WWJD. For some reason, we as a society have become quite fond of that question. I'm not sure what brought about the Holy uproar, but it caught on faster than "all that", "talk to the hand" or the thankfully retired "get jiggy with it".

Unlike all of the other catchphrases we've introduced into the lexicon, this one seems to have a more significant meaning. Just the mere mention of our Lord and Savior elevates this one to the next level. I mean, when you here the name Jesus, it automatically changes the importance of whatever it is you're talking about. For example, I could go out right now and start marketing "What would KJ do?" bracelets, and even though it may be fun to wonder what KJ would do in any number of situations, I don't know if the bracelets would be flying off the shelves. But there's something about the name of Jesus that changes everything.

I first noticed this a few years ago. Wherever you looked, you saw the initials WWJD. Some knew what it meant and others were clueless. But over time, we all became aware of that question. It seems simple enough, and yet the more you think about it, the more complicated it becomes. It's not so much about figuring out what Jesus would do in any particular situation, but to answer that question causes another, more personal question. To know what Jesus would do, you simply need to consult a Bible. After getting an idea of what Jesus would do, one has to ask oneself another question: What will I do?

Wanna buy a t-shirt?

I can't help but think that this phrase first came about because someone wanted to improve mankind's relationship with itself. Someone wanted to give us something that would make us stop when we're angry, when we see our fellow man in need of help or when just living our day to day lives. In those situations, we were to stop and ask ourselves, "What would Jesus do?" Sounds like an awesome idea. If we can't check ourselves in the name of decency, then let's use the example set by Jesus. Not that it's a bad thing to do that, because we should all use Jesus as a role model and example of how we should live our lives. But do we need a rubber bracelet to carry the Son of God's example with us?

Over the last few years, these bracelets, license plate holders, t-shirts, coffee mugs and whatever else this phrase finds itself on has taken on a new life. What started out as a message to all of us to stop and think about what we do to one another in our daily lives quickly became a fashion statement. Before you knew it, you were seeing WWJD everywhere. Something that would supposedly be reserved for the Christian portion of our society (or at the very least, the righteous) was now being seen everywhere. Even people who only come to church on Easter Sunday could be overheard uttering that phrase as if they knew the answer. I mean, in their world, Jesus would put on a brand new suit and show up once a year.

And I'm sure we've got a few die-hards out there who take the whole thing to a completely different extreme. These are usually the same people that try to live the Bible of yesterday, today. If you commit adultery, they still think we should stone you to death, even though that's considered barbaric these days. These are the same people that think God only speaks to us through burning shrubbery. They won't even cook dinner without asking "What would Jesus cook?"

Just like so many other things in our society, once the phrase and the bracelets and such became popular, it became more of the cool thing to do or say. No one really focused on the meaning anymore. No one really thought about what they were asking anymore. It was what everybody was doing, or in this case, saying. At the same time, just like everything else that has a significant meaning or message behind it, once it became mainstream, this phrase got watered down and lost some of its power. People that were new to the concept of Jesus and what He'd actually do in any particular situation were beginning to latch on to the WWJD phenomenon simply because they saw it everywhere. Judging by what we still see in the world and how we're still treated by some of our so-called friends, families, fellow church members and neighbors, some of us are embracing WWJD for show. Even those that actually know what Jesus would do are still reluctant to follow His lead.

We as a society are always quick to embrace anything that's popular, most times without even investigating what we're embracing. If you don't know the history of something, you can take it in the wrong direction. If you don't know the history of something, you wind up embracing something that you have no idea about. Once the world wraps its arms around something, more times than not, it goes in the wrong direction. This was a question that was supposed to change our thinking, yet in true capitalistic fashion, we saw an opportunity for profit and slapped it on anything that we could and began to sell, sell, sell!

Now, I don't want anybody to think I'm against earning a living. As I've said before, I hope you bought this book as opposed to borrowing a friend's. I just wish that we were actually selling the message of what Jesus would do as opposed to selling a "catchphrase" or a cool monogram. I long for the day that Jesus will be "cool" in the eyes of all. But I want it to be for the right reasons. I want it to be for what Jesus represents and not because somebody wears a particular t-shirt because they want me to think that they really care about their fellow man. I want what Jesus would do to matter simply because it *does* matter and not because of a brilliant marketing scheme.

Losing my religion

As I stated earlier, to ask what Jesus would do actually requires a little soul searching on one's part. First, if you have to ask what Jesus would do, you're kind of admitting that you either don't know or you do and don't quite follow it all of the time. Most of us tend to be in the latter portion of that statement. We all have a sense of right and wrong, but we don't always follow the path of the righteous. So this question exists for a lot of us as a guideline on how we *should* be living our lives.

At the same time, this question exists because of another reality. In most cases, what we would do is either not good enough or not even the right thing to do. This question seems to have come about out of necessity. Like we needed a reminder of what was the right way to handle certain situations in our lives. It almost seems that mankind could no longer count on its own sense of morality when dealing with one another, so we had to come up with something to make us stop and think before we just act and react.

Every day of our lives, we're put to the test in one way or another. You may have a friend or family member in need. You may be tempted to cheat on your spouse. You may be tempted to skip church. Or maybe you've been pushed too far on your job and you're tempted to use a few four letter words to let someone know how you feel about it. Maybe you have a choice between dishonesty and the truth. Maybe you're trying to decide whether to tithe or keep what belongs to God for yourself. There could be a situation where you have a choice between taking advantage of your fellow man and doing the right thing. Or, perhaps, maybe you have a choice between truly protecting the people you were elected to protect and sending their children off to fight an unjust war. When situations like this arise, what would you do?

For the most part, we have yet to learn to get along here on earth. We also haven't learned the joy of giving of ourselves to those less fortunate. We don't even know how to truly and unconditionally love one another. When faced with the opportunity to make a positive impact on another individual or on the world, we sometimes come up with the most negative behavior. Take some of the situations I listed in the last paragraph. With the exception of one, all of us have probably been there a time or two. How many of us have taken the negative rather than the positive? All of us have.

Some of us will go to church (or wherever your house of worship may be) every Sunday and yet we're still willing to let somebody know what time it is, using the most colorful language that we can. Does that make us bad people? Of course not. Is that the way that we should be? Again, of course not. Though not right, it's just a part of being human. None of us are perfect and we're here to do the best that we can. I'm just not so sure that we're always doing the best that we can.

What would you do if you caught your husband or wife cheating on you? Would you sit down and talk it out or would you grab your gun and shoot it out? What if you found out that your best friend was talking about you behind your back? Would you be more inclined to curse him or her out or talk it out? What about church? What if you felt that leadership was lacking in your place of worship? Would you sit down with your pastor and express your feelings on the matter or would you join a group of modern day Pharisees that sits back, criticizes and gossips about the situation? In short, are you part of the problem or are you, like Jesus, a part of the solution?

Before asking what Jesus would do, we all need to take a long look at ourselves. We need to get ourselves to a place where what we do and how we treat one another is something natural as opposed to our behavior being the answer to a question. At the same time, we can't allow that question to become rhetorical in our lives. The question "What would Jesus do?" begs to be answered. But when the question is asked, are we able to answer? Are we capable of doing what Jesus would do while we're still in the flesh?

If you know anything about Jesus, then you know something about yourself. We all come from the same lineage, so to speak. We are all God's children. When Jesus took on the flesh, He became susceptible to the same things that we're susceptible to. The pains that the human body feels, the emotions that we feel and even the temptations that we face on a day to day basis. Though He was God's son and He could heal the sick and raise the dead, He was still human. We need no more proof than to know that He died on Calvary. Though we're not capable of rising from the grave on the third day, what Jesus showed us while He lived in the flesh was that we are capable of being like Him, though we exist in the flesh.

When Jesus went into the wilderness to fast, he was tempted by the devil. He was shown all that He could possess if He would simply bow down to Satan. Because the spirit was strong, He was able to resists the temptations of the flesh. We have that same ability, even though we're not always so willing to put it into practice. Jesus was also capable of the anger that we're all so willing to display. If you look at Matthew 21:12, you will see where Jesus went into the temple and drove out the moneychangers who turned God's house into a "den of thieves". The Bible also says that He overturned their tables. I doubt that was done gently. And yet, even in His anger, His heart was in the right place and His mind was on what God would have Him do. How many of us bracelet wearers can say that?

A change has gotta come

If we really want to do what Jesus would do, every one of us has a lot of changing to do. I don't know all of you personally, but I'm sure that all of us are falling short of the glory these days. In order to reach the promise of those classy bracelets we wear, we have to tear down some things that are very much a part of us. Some of us just need a little tweaking. However, most of us are in need of a major, major overhaul. I'm honest enough to say that I'm in the major category.

What often happens when we've realized that we're in need of change is the initial tweak. We always want to change a little here, and a little there, when in fact, we need a big change here and a humongous change over there. It's natural to want to take baby steps, or implement the change in small doses. The mistake that we make, however, is a simple one. It's alright to take baby steps, as long as we realize that they are steps to a goal. When we tweak, we usually stop. We only go as far as we want to go, but usually don't go as far as we need to go.

Let me give you some examples. If you're a drinker and you know anything about the Bible, then you know that the Bible speaks out against alcohol. If you're a drinker and you *think* you know something about the Bible and you don't think the Bible does actually speak out against alcohol, then let me enlighten you just a bit.

Wine is a mocker, strong drink is raging: and whosoever is deceived thereby is not wise
— Proverbs 20:1

134

Now some of you are confused by that. Some of you drinking Bible students are still thinking about the Second Chapter of John when Jesus went to a wedding and turned water into wine. He must have been in favor of keeping the party live, right? Not so fast, my friend. We're in a bit of a gray area. The Proverbs verse doesn't necessarily say that one shouldn't drink at all. What I think that verse is saying is that some things we do in our lives, we wind up overdoing. That verse is speaking about the abuse of alcohol and how it is unwise to abuse our bodies in that way. That's where the deception is. Not knowing when to say when. Not knowing when enough is enough. In short, not being able to drink in moderation. That verse is for all who drink to get drunk.

I never have, and hopefully through the grace of God, never will be a drinker. Not looking down my nose at those who do, but it's just a choice that I've made. I don't think that we have to shun alcohol in all its forms. However, there has been many a bad decision made due to not controlling one's alcohol intake. Where God may not frown upon our desire to eat, drink and be merry, I don't think he wants us to eat, get drunk and try to do Mary. Jesus didn't turn that water into wine with the mindset that it ain't no party like a Cana party 'cause a Cana party don't stop. And you can best believe that folks were on their best behavior because the Son of God was in the house.

What Jesus was doing was performing one of his many miracles to come. He was showing how God was working through Him. Yet, I'm sure that there's no record of Jesus staggering home after the wedding because He had too much of His own "liquor". If we really are looking to Jesus as an example, you can look at that fact. Just because there was strong drink available doesn't mean that He had to partake. Just because others were doing it, doesn't mean that He had to do it. Now, I know that Jesus was special and though He was in the flesh, He was still the Son of God. But we all have that same ability that Jesus had to say no.

Yet, when some of us are faced with the opportunity to at the very least temper our alcohol intake, a lot of us seem to have trouble with it. We know we need to change, but we're not willing to do what it takes. We know we need to stop drinking as much as we do, but we won't stay out of the night clubs where drinking is their business and keeping the drinks flowing is not a miracle of God, but rather how they keep the lights on.

We know that alcohol leads to a lot of poor decisions that we make, but we get drunk, use poor judgment, and drive. We get drunk, use poor judgment, and have unprotected sex. We get drunk, use poor judgment, and have protected sex, but with people that we have no business having sex with. We get drunk and say or do mean and hurtful things to people that we claim to love. Yet, in this situation, we never ask that question: What would Jesus do?

If you're a drinker, please don't think that I'm saying that you should never, ever drink. Hopefully, you haven't slammed my book shut in disgust. I'm not speaking to those of you that know how to do this in moderation. Again, I'm speaking to those that get drunk. I'm speaking to those that can't stop themselves. I'm speaking to those that have done unspeakable things (whether they remember them or not) because they were drunk. I'm speaking to those that have done these things and still don't have the good sense to stop.

For those that are trying to stop, you need to understand that breaking this chain isn't something that you can do by "tweaking", as I talked about earlier. It's just like any other addiction. You can't go to the same places that you used to go. You can't do what you used to do. And, in some cases, you can't hang around the same people that you used to hang around with. However, some of us think it's as simple as not going here or not drinking that or not seeing that person anymore.

What's usually needed is a fundamental change in who we are as individuals. You have to change your core. If you don't do that, then the same desires exist and the potential to do the things that you used to do is more prevalent than it would be if you don't change that core. When we change who we are, then certain things don't make sense to do anymore. When we change who we are, certain desires will fade away. You can change your surroundings all you want, but if you don't change you, then your pitfalls await you. If we're really trying to get ourselves in line with what Jesus would do, then we have to be committed to the idea. That's always easier said on a t-shirt than done.

Maybe you should take off your bracelet before we do this...

What about the sex that I mentioned earlier? Again, almost all of us have fallen short, myself included. If you don't have a spouse, then you're outside of the will of God. Does that mean we stop? Most times, no. Sometimes, it's the result of the alcohol that I spoke about earlier. In most cases, a drunken mind is unable to make a sober choice. So when we should be practicing restraint, we're unable to because we aren't fully in control of our faculties. But for some, that's a crutch. They feel that they can be excused of certain behavior because they weren't in their right minds when they made the mistake. In that case, it would seem that making a seemingly conscience choice to fornicate is worse than making one under the influence. However, one has to remember that being drunk and fornicating are two problems, not one. But, I digress.

Our desire to have sex whether married or not, is similar to the drinker's desire to drink until he's drunk. When it goes unchecked, we will sometimes do it to our detriment. The major difference is that we can have a drink or two in moderation and still be in the will of God. There's no fornication in the will of God. Does that mean that you will, to quote my late Uncle Mack, "bust hell wide open"? No, because the God we serve is forgiving. Does that mean that it's okay to continue on the way we are? No, because God is not pleased when we do. And just like our addiction to alcohol, we can correct that situation. Alcoholics can get treatment, and fornicators can get married. So which is worse and where do we begin?

Let's start with which is supposedly worse. In our quest to uncover what Jesus would do, we mustn't get to a place where we begin to measure our sins. God is not pleased with *any* of our sins. We as a society have placed such a stigma on sex that a man and his wife can barely enjoy sex without feeling the need to repent afterwards. If there's anything in our society that has a million faces, it's sex. We've gotten so out of control with sex that it's on every corner, TV screen, magazine cover, and in just about every song that we listen to. We have become desensitized to the point where we don't know when to be shocked, embarrassed, ashamed or whatever. At the same time, the conservatives have become even more conservative, refusing to even acknowledge the existence of sex and its natural place in our lives.

What this leads to is us judging one another based on how we perceive sex. Try this at your church: Renew your membership because you have sinned against your brother by cheating him out of some money and you feel that when you took advantage of him, you broke the church covenant and fell out of fellowship with the church. See how many strange looks you get from people because they think you're taking this whole church thing too seriously and you're overreacting to something small that you could've settled by simply returning the money and saying "I'm sorry".

Now, try to use that "I'm sorry" method when you get pregnant out of wedlock. If you were raised in the Baptist church, then you're familiar with what I'm talking about. A girl gets pregnant out of wedlock, and she's expected to renew her membership because she's broken the church covenant. Now, most people think it's because she's pregnant. No, that's not it. It's because she's had sex, she has no husband and there's no way to hide it anymore. Would a woman be able to just say "I'm sorry" in this situation? No sir or madam. Because judgment doesn't come like it's supposed to, from God. Judgment comes from here on earth.

This is where a practice that I call sin measurement comes into play. I can use all types of foul language, but you'd better not get pregnant out of wedlock. I can cheat, steal and lie on my fellow man, but I'd better not hear that you've been out there having sex. I can dishonor my parents and disrespect the man of God each Sunday at church, but the rumor is that you're out there having sex, so at least I'm not as bad as you. Amongst all of our everyday sins, sex has become the super sin.

It's a human reaction for us to separate what we do into degrees. We're conditioned by the society that we live in. We have laws in the Christian world that we have to govern ourselves by, but there are laws in the secular world as well. The punishments for shoplifting and drunk driving can't be the same. The punishments for writing bad checks and breaking and entering can't be the same. The punishments for aggravated assault and first degree murder can't be the same. All of these crimes vary in degree of severity, so the punishments vary in degree (putting aside our knowledge that sometimes the system does fail and sometimes these violations go unpunished).

Because we have been conditioned to measure violations by the society that we live, we have begun to measure out our sins as well. I have to believe that all of the Commandments that God gave to Moses, outside of having no other gods before him, were of equal importance. But in our human nature, we only take some seriously. To us, the others are there as a guideline, but not really that pertinent. Because we have taken sex to the front of the sin line, even ahead of murder in some cases, we fornicators have begun to think that if we can just eliminate that from our lives, we're on our way to Heaven for sure.

But again, I caution you. What about the language we use? What about the lies we tell? What about the fact that you'll skip church when there's nothing physically wrong with you? What about our unwillingness to tithe as we should? What about our judgment of one another? What about the disrespect that we show our parents? What about the excessive drinking that we've already talked about? What about that "little bit of weed" that we smoke as if it's okay? What about the false commitment that we show to God, as if He can be fooled? What about us not really knowing what Jesus would do?

If it seems like I'm calling for perfection, don't get me wrong. Only someone who's lived in imperfection can write these words, and I'm no saint. It's just that I've noticed that we as humans always think that we're one or two sins from being perfect and on the right path. If I could just stop all of the sex, I'm there. If I could just stop all of the drinking, I'm there. If I could just stop all of the swearing, I'm there. Nothing could be further from the truth. We were born into sin. No matter what, you'll always be doing something wrong. You'll never be all the way there. That's one reason why God is so forgiving. Because He almost has to be or He's gonna be pretty lonely up there. If only those with a completely spotless record get into Heaven, none of us are going home.

That doesn't mean that we should stop trying. We should never give up on trying to do what's right. We don't give up on anything else. We never stop trying to find that perfect high, that perfect sex partner, that perfect car that's out of our means, that perfect hustle (whether your hustle is in the street sense or the club sense; we black folks can come up with some dance steps, can't we?) or the perfect lie to mask the fact that we do all of the things I've just mentioned. I believe that we were put here to be Christ-like in our ways. I also believe that we never completely achieve that before we die, but we are expected to do the best that we can.

I believe that God has given us a blueprint on how we are supposed to live and He sent His Son, not only to die for our sins, but to show us His blueprint in the flesh. Because God is God, He knows what each of us are and aren't capable of. I think the expectation is for us to try to live right and treat each other right while we're here. "What would Jesus do?" is a great question. "What would I do?" is a better question. But "What am I doing?" is probably the most difficult question of all. If we're being honest, the answer isn't always that flattering. I don't think God wants us to beat ourselves up over everything that we do wrong. Most times, we know when we're doing wrong, and that's a start. All of the sins we commit are correctable. For that reason, we should try to correct them. If you drink to get drunk, get some help. If you're sleeping with someone that you're not married to, maybe you should think about marriage. If you have a problem with honesty, maybe it's time to check yourself.

However, let's not forget what we talked about earlier in this chapter. Baby steps. Most of us fall short because we wake up one day and decide that we're going to be Super Christians or Super Righteous and change everything right now, once and for all. You can quit some things cold turkey, but other things take time. Most of the sins we commit have some element to them that feels really good or that we enjoy greatly on some level. If they didn't, we wouldn't be doing them. So in order to give them up, we have to give up something that we really enjoy. That's not always the easiest thing to do and it will take some time. Think of how much damage drugs and alcohol will do to some before they realize why they need to give it up. And sometimes it's too late when they finally do. The same can be said about sex, especially the unprotected variety.

Any major change in your life will take some time. Getting yourself to that point where you can just react without having to stop and ask questions about Jesus will take some time. You have to be patient. Once you realize that change is necessary, then make a plan and implement it. Don't be discouraged because you fall short every once in a while. Those who succeed at anything don't succeed because they never fall down. They succeed because when they do fall down, the always get up and keep going.

How long are you planning to hold that grudge?

What about forgiveness? With all of the sinning that we do, we spend a lot of time looking for forgiveness from God. Although this is what we're taught to do, we're never as willing to forgive others that trespass against us. Some of us can hold grudges for years and years, simply because we think we're right. Sometimes we don't show the proper perspective in certain situations. Some things are a matter of right and wrong, and some things are a matter of opinion. If it's a matter of opinion, who's really wrong? We have to have the ability to agree to disagree without having a situation turn into a long running feud.

Like a lot of things talked about in this chapter, forgiveness is something that we need to practice daily. It can do a lot in the way of relieving stress in your life. Rather than walking around with malice and anger in your heart, you can walk around with a sense of calm. We have the opportunity to practice this everyday. Instead of not speaking to your brother or sister because of that argument at the last barbeque, how about calling them up and telling them that you love them? Instead of yelling and cursing at that man that just cut you off on the freeway, how about just showing a little restraint? Honestly, is it really that serious if no one was hurt? How 'bout just letting it go instead of giving that middle finger of yours a workout. After all, if Jesus drove in His day, that's what He would do.

There used to be a mentality that existed that we shouldn't let the sun go down on our anger. We're so bad now, that seasons change on our anger. We've lost sight of the fact that all of us are sick enough to die right now and we don't always have tomorrow to settle differences that we should settle today. I've known people that will stop speaking to me for weeks and months at a time because of my honesty and my unwillingness to sugar coat my feelings at times. They won't call me because they think I was wrong, and I won't call them because I think I was right. Neither of us are in the right. Although we both have the right to stand our ground, how we handle the situation is all wrong. We let pride dictate how we treat one another.

We have to learn to forgive one another for our own sake. It doesn't matter who's right or wrong. We fall short because we're human and emotion takes over sometimes. I'm trying each day to become a better person, but it doesn't always work. I'm trying each day not to be angry for two and three weeks about something somebody said or didn't say to me. I realize first hand that its easier said than done. Sometimes people can make us so mad, but we have to have perspective. We have to have the ability to recognize our own faults. We're just as capable of making somebody else mad. We're just as capable of being as wrong as we think they are. If you feel that someone has mistreated you, you should let them know. Maybe they don't realize it, or maybe they do but they don't realize how it's affecting you. At the end of the day, no matter how they feel, you need to find it in your heart to forgive them anyway. Not only to clear your conscience, but because it's the right thing to do. Put that into practice and see how your life changes.

In addition to that, most of us continue to be ungrateful. We've yet to learn that we should appreciate what we have instead of always complaining about what we don't have. I once told a friend that was constantly complaining about how life isn't fair to her to try going out and doing something for someone less fortunate the next time she feels that way. I told her that it would give her perspective. Things are never as bad as we make them seem. God has blessed some of us with homes and transportation, and sometimes we make just enough on our jobs to cover the bills. Instead of seeing the blessing in being able to support ourselves, though barely, all we can do is complain about the fact that we're "barely makin' it". Well, there are homeless people out there that would love to be "barely makin' it" the way that we are.

We have to learn to give of ourselves. And we have to be selfless when we give. We can't do it just because there's something in it for us. We can't do it in order to get something in return. We can't do it so that someone can owe us a favor. We have to learn to give from the heart. We will never know true happiness unless we do. You'll never receive the fullness of God's blessing if you won't assist Him in blessing someone else. You'll never receive true love unless you learn to give true love to someone else. You can't do what Jesus would do if you won't do anything for anyone else without expecting something in return.

Let's stand for the benediction...

In the end, we all have the ability to do what Jesus would do. But if you wear one of those bracelets or t-shirts or drink from a coffee cup with that question on it, then that means that you probably already believe in Jesus. And if you already believe in Jesus, then you should already know what Jesus would do. And chances are it's nowhere near what you would do. If you know your Bible, then there's never a question of what Jesus would do. It's all about being the best person that you can be. Not perfect, but the best that you can be. Jesus can be the benchmark for what we want to be, but don't be discouraged if you don't quite get there sometimes. It's all a part of the process. To quote a song by the group Groove Theory, which featured the fabulous Amel Larriuex: "Lift your head to the sky and keep trying/ believe in you, and it will take you higher". You can't do what Jesus would do if Jesus ain't in you.

Whoever decided to coin this phrase was simply trying to improve us as a people. I believe they wanted us to take a look at how we were treating one another. It's not always the best. I believe the thought was, if we all stopped and asked that question before reacting to one another, then maybe our reactions would improve, and thus society would improve. And in the event that someone who didn't know Jesus were asking that question, then I'm sure the hope was that they would educate themselves on the life and times of Jesus Christ. Because in reality, the question isn't "What would Jesus do?", the question is "What has Jesus already done?". The reality is that whatever Jesus would do in any of our modern situations, He's already done.

If you're of the Christian faith, then you know that we should all strive to be Christ-like in our lives. Jesus is an example for us. He was the ultimate role model. The question "What would Jesus do?" suggests that. We ask what Jesus would do, and yet He's already lived the answer for us. Would Jesus drink excessively? Of course not. Would Jesus fornicate? Of course not. Would Jesus lie? No sir or madam. Even though we don't exist in the same time in which Jesus existed, His example remains the same, and thus what He would do remains the same.

If He was mistreated by His fellow man, He would forgive him. If you don't believe me, look to Calvary. If He were tempted by the devil, He'd resist that temptation. Don't believe me? Ask that same devil that tried to tempt Him. Those of us that believe in Jesus already know what Jesus would do because we already know what He's done. The question exists for us only as a novelty. It's all about your individual relationship with God. That should be what shapes your behavior. That should be what makes us treat one another right. Not a bracelet. Not a question. Now having said all of that, only one question remains: Going forward, when life presents you with that moral dilemma, what will you do?

About the author

Kelly R. Jackson has been an author/poet for over 20 years. He published his first book, *Temporarily Disconnected*, in 2006. His second book, *Scenes From The Blue Book*, was published in 2007. He's the father of one son and he is a native of Detroit, Michigan, where he still resides. He is also a member of Zion Hill Baptist Church on Detroit's east side.

To contact Kelly R. Jackson, read more of his work or to give feedback on any of his projects, visit www.kjworldonline.com or email him at kjworld@kjworldonline.com.